SECRET NORTHWEST INDIANA

A Guide to the Weird, Wonderful, and Obscure

Joseph S. Pete

Copyright © 2022, Reedy Press, LLC
All rights reserved.

Reedy Press
PO Box 5131
St. Louis, MO 63139
www.reedypress.com

Library of Congress Control Number: 2021950869
ISBN: 9781681063669

Design by Jill Halpin

Unless otherwise indicated, all photos are courtesy of the author or in the public domain.

Printed in the United States of America
22 23 24 25 26   5 4 3 2 1

For Harper

CONTENTS

ACKNOWLEDGMENTS

The author would like to express his boundless gratitude to everyone who assisted him with researching and writing this book. His appreciation dates back to his parents Robert and Judy and the value they placed on reading and education, all of his teachers over the years, and his professors at Indiana University, especially those who saw any glint of promise in him. Special thanks go to the Lake County Public Library, *The Times of Northwest Indiana* archives, and museums across Northwest Indiana both large and small. Thanks go to previous Northwest Indiana authors like James Lane, Norma Schaeffer, Kay Franklin, Robert Flood, Kenneth J. Brock, and Kenneth J. Schoon, and that long-haired kid who was gracious enough to give the author a tour of the paintball field just before it closed. Books like *Weird Indiana* and *Oddball Indiana* and websites like Atlas Obscura and Orange Bean Indiana proved helpful, at least as a starting point for how to approach the book's subject matter. He is of course very grateful to his wife and editor Meredith, without whom this book wouldn't have been possible.

INTRODUCTION

A blend of big-city Chicago and downstate Indiana, the Region has drawn many comparisons over the years. With hulking steel mills along the Lake Michigan shore, it's been described as "Pittsburgh and steel's lovechild." It was compared to Germany's mighty Ruhr Valley during its industrial heyday. It's been likened to Detroit and other Rust Belt burghs as industry started to decline. Its sweeping sand dunes stood in for the Sahara Desert in silent films. But there really is no place like the Calumet Region. Stretching from Chicago's far South Side and the south suburbs in Illinois through several counties in Northwest Indiana to Southwest Michigan, the Region is one of a kind. The Indiana Dunes boast some of the greatest biodiversity in the United States with seas of wildflowers, lush green forests, and prickly cacti. Migratory birds flock from across North America to Northwest Indiana because of the inland ocean of Lake Michigan, which also brings huge ocean-going ships from around the world. Its steel mills, oil refineries, and factories keep America running but also rank among the country's worst polluters. Its ethnic diversity remains so great that it's not unusual to hear people talking in other languages, including Polish. It's home to 24-hour fireworks stores, drive-through smoke shops, and many other oddities. In this book, I set out to chronicle much of what's weird and wonderful in Northwest Indiana. I ventured all across the Region from city to farm, going on adventures, falling in the mud, and even getting kicked out of a few places. I snapped plenty of pictures of everything from graffiti murals to Great Blue Herons taking flight to human skulls found on a serial killer's farm. The Region has a rich but sometimes secret history this book seeks to unveil. So, get out there. Carpe diem. Carpe Region.

WHERE JOHN DILLINGER ESCAPED FROM JAIL

Where did John Dillinger escape from an "escape-proof" jail?

The infamous gangster John Dillinger, Public Enemy No. 1, became more legend than man after his bank robberies were breathlessly sensationalized by huge-font headlines in newspapers that cast him as a populist Robin Hood figure during the Great Depression—a time when banks were at the nadir of their popularity. Just months after his release from the Indiana State Prison in Michigan City, he was arrested for the murder of Patrolman William Patrick O'Malley during a bank robbery in East Chicago. O'Malley shot Dillinger in a gunfight but hit his bulletproof vest. The Dillinger Gang's leader, the most wanted man in America, was arrested in Arizona and extradited to a supposedly escape-proof jail in Crown Point. He made his notorious escape by whittling a wooden gun, taking guards hostage, and stealing Sheriff Lillian Holley's police car before abandoning it in nearby Chicago. "If I ever see John Dillinger, I'll shoot him dead with my own pistol," she told *Time Magazine*.

You can see the cell Dillinger occupied and where he locked up 14 jailers at The Old Lake County Sheriff's House and Jail in downtown Crown Point. Al Capone hitman James "Fur" Sammons was also once imprisoned there. The county jail was moved in 1974, but preservationists restored the original 1882

Knowledgeable docents lead groups on tours of the jail from early May through late December, showing visitors where and how one of history's most daring escapes happened before it became the stuff of public lore.

Wooden Gun
Owned by Tony Stewart

COLT 38

JOHN DILLINGER'S WOODEN GUN
Dillinger Museum Replica
March 3, 1934

Top left: *John Dillinger was imprisoned in the Old Lake County Jail but not for long.*

Top right: *Public Enemy #1 whittled a gun out of wood, banked on his fearsome reputation, and bluffed better than any poker player to make one of the most famous escapes in history.*

Above left: *The bank-robbing gangster John Dillinger escaped from the Old Lake County Jail with a wooden gun.*

OLD SHERIFF'S HOUSE AND JAIL

WHAT: Site of John Dillinger's infamous jailbreak

WHERE: 226 S Main St., Crown Point, IN

COST: $5 for adults, $2 for children 6-12, $10 for haunted house

PRO TIP: The Indiana Ghost Trackers' annual Chaos Haunted and Historic Bus Tour stops by the Crown Point Jail and other supposedly haunted spots like the Kahler Middle School in Dyer and the Kaske House.

jail and got it listed on the National Register of Historic Places. Featured in the Johnny Depp movie *Public Enemies* that was filmed in downtown Crown Point, the old jail is now a history museum that offers guided tours during the summer and the popular Criminally Insane haunted house before Halloween. It hosts regular events throughout the year, including ghost tours, music video shoots, and gangster-themed weddings. Many artifacts are on display, including the wooden gun, vintage newspapers with screaming headlines, and a death mask of Dillinger from after FBI agents gunned him down outside the Biograph Theater in Chicago.

DIANA OF THE DUNES'S OLD STOMPING GROUNDS

What about the Indiana Dunes captivated Diana of the Dunes so?

Diana of the Dunes, née Alice Mabel Gray, blazed a path as a legendary free-spirited bohemian whose advocacy helped save part of the Indiana Dunes from encroaching development. The iconic figure who graduated from the University of Chicago gave up a comfortable life in the city to subsist alone in an abandoned shanty she dubbed "Driftwood" in the wilds of the dunes in the early 1900s. The nonconformist lived a simplified, solitary existence by the beach, where she read and wrote about the dunes' natural history. Her eccentric lifestyle made her a local folk legend, drawing curiosity seekers, gawker-filled tour boats, and media attention that sometimes sensationalized her as a young nymph who skinny-dipped in Lake Michigan. The Lake County Times described her as "the most interesting person living in Northern Indiana." A stirring speech she gave to the Chicago Prairie Club at the Art Institute of Chicago helped generate interest in saving the Indiana Dunes at a time when they were being strip-mined for commercial interests like Ball Jars and building foundations.

Her passion is credited with ultimately leading to the creation of the Indiana Dunes State Park and the Indiana Dunes National Park that together draw around 3 million visitors per

DIANA OF THE DUNES DARE TRAIL

WHAT: Diana of the Dunes's old stomping grounds

WHERE: West Beach, 376 N County Line Rd., Gary, IN

COST: $6 for parking during the beach season between Memorial Day and Labor Day, free the rest of the year

PRO TIP: Get there early in the summer to find parking, as space is limited and it's the most popular beach in the Indiana Dunes National Park.

Top: *The Diana of the Dunes Dare, formerly the Dunes Succession Trail, leads one through the wild, untrammeled landscape she devoted her life to.*

Inset: *The Diana of the Dunes Dare takes one up 270 wooden stairs to the top of a dune where one can see Lake Michigan and the Chicago skyline.*

year. The bohemian who lived attuned to nature has been forever immortalized on the former Succession Trail on West Beach. It was rebranded in 2021 as the Diana of the Dunes Dare in her honor and to capitalize on the popularity of the Three Dunes Challenge at the neighboring Indiana Dunes State Park. The mile-long trail illustrates the phases of dunes succession as it progresses from beachfront to heavy vegetation like marram grass, wild blueberries, and cottonwood trees. It's a strenuous but scenic trek past blowouts, flowering plants, and interdunal ponds with some spectacular views at the top.

The hike from the main West Beach parking lot up hundreds of wooden stairs features interpretative signs and a breathtaking view of Lake Michigan roaring off in the distance from the top of Diana's Dune.

SHIPWRECK AT THE BOTTOM OF LAKE MICHIGAN

Why does Lake Michigan have so many shipwrecks?

Lake Michigan's South Shore is littered with shipwrecks, with 50 alone just off the Indiana shoreline, largely because most date back to a more primitive and dangerous time of maritime navigation when it was more central to interstate commerce. That figure doesn't even include ships that were lost and never found or scavenged by the shore and broken up by the tide. An estimated 2,000 ships ranging from single-masted vessels to wooden steamers have gone missing on Lake Michigan since commercial shipping took off in the 1800s but only a small number of them were ever found.

You can visit the underwater wreckage of a ship that sank in 1911 in the *J.D. Marshall* Nature Preserve about a half-mile off the shore in the Indiana Dunes State Park. The 100-acre state-dedicated nature preserve is marked by buoys. Extending down 30 feet to the lake bed, it protects the 154-foot-long channeler vessel that was built in South Haven, Michigan, in 1891 to haul goods like lumber. While carrying 1,000 tons of sand to a Chicago glass factory, the ship capsized—"turned turtle" in sailor parlance—during a squall that bombarded it with 20-foot-

You can either scuba dive or snorkel to the shipwreck. Scuba gear can be rented from Goose's Scuba Shack in Dyer or Lake County Divers Supply in downtown Hobart. The Indiana Department of Natural Resources also offers virtual tours online.

Top: *The propeller of the* J.D. Marshall *sits as a memorial on Porter Beach not far from where the ship sunk off the shoreline.*

Inset: *Wreckage from the shipwreck can be viewed at the Indiana Dunes State Park Nature Center.*

J.D. MARSHALL NATURE PRESERVE

WHAT: Shipwreck off Lake Michigan coast

WHERE: 1600 N 25 E, Chesterton, IN

COST: $7 for in-state, $12 for out-of-state

PRO TIP: Bring an underwater compass and don't go after heavy rain when outfall from local rivers clouds the underwater visibility.

tall waves just off the shore in Porter County. Four of the 10 crew members died in what was one of Indiana's largest maritime disasters. The first mate's watch stopped at 1:45 a.m., the time he was dispatched to a watery grave. Scavengers were caught by the US Coast Guard trying to raise the *J.D. Marshall* in the 1980s, spurring preservation efforts. You can scuba dive to the wreckage just off the beach. Landlubbers can see the engine propeller on the east side of the historic pavilion and the ship's recreated pilothouse inside the Nature Center.

Another shipwreck close to shore is the SS *Muskegon* in Michigan City. Its tale is far less tragic. It caught fire in the harbor and was dragged out into Lake Michigan and sunk by residents who were sick of looking at the burnt-out hull.

SUBMARINES UNDER LAKE MICHIGAN

Where can you learn about experimental submarines once tested in Lake Michigan?

Indiana is generally thought of as landlocked, an endless flat expanse of corn stalks and soybeans in the bland and topographically unvarying Midwest. But the northwest corner of the state has a robust maritime history given its position on a Great Lake, where the Indiana coastline stretches for 45 miles along the South Shore of Lake Michigan. Iron ore boats haul raw materials to the steel mills. Hulking international vessels called salties pass through the St. Lawrence Seaway from the Atlantic Ocean en route to the Port of Indiana-Burns Harbor. The Old Lighthouse Museum chronicles the nautical history, including shipwrecks in Lake Michigan, maritime disasters, ships that sailed from Michigan City's harbor, and the Showboat Dixiana where the play *Tobacco Road* was staged.

The museum operates out of Michigan City's 1858 lighthouse that has since been replaced as a functioning beacon with the now-iconic lighthouse out in the lake. You can still clamber up the narrow stairs to peer out of the old lantern room. One of the more unusual stories from there was of submarine inventor Lodner Darvantis Phillips, a Michigan City shoemaker who pioneered submarines on the Great Lakes. Phillips designed and built several submarines, taking his family on underwater picnics and attempting to salvage

OLD LIGHTHOUSE MUSEUM

WHAT: Maritime museum in a historic lighthouse

WHERE: 1 Washington St., Michigan City, IN

COST: $5 for adults, $2 for children under 14

PRO TIP: Don't miss the exhibit about Lincoln's funeral train stopping through town.

Left: *Dive into the history of submarines on the Great Lakes at the Old Lighthouse Museum in Michigan City.*

Right: *Lodner Darvantis Phillips never sold a submarine to the Navy but his cigar-shaped design proved widely influential.*

wrecks. In the 1840s, he reputedly sank one of the models, known as the Fool Killer or the Marine Cigar, on a test run in the Chicago River. He never realized his dream of selling a submarine design to the Navy but is credited with launching the first submarine to sail the Great Lakes in 1851 near the old lighthouse. A plaque outside commemorates the occasion. There's an exhibit dedicated to Phillips's underwater exploits in Lake Michigan in the seafaring, memorabilia-crammed museum that author Ray Boomhauer noted "still manages to shed light on the historic past of the city and life on the lake."

Indiana's only lighthouse was kept lit for 40 years by Harriet Colfax, a cousin of vice president Schuyler Colfax. The lightkeeper made arduous nightly trips to replenish the lamp's oil, a dangerous trek when Lake Michigan froze over in the winter.

BELLE GUNNESS EXHIBIT

How did "one of the most prolific serial killers in American history" claim her victims?

Belle Gunness is immortalized forever at the La Porte County Historical Society Museum and by ballads she inspired. The notorious Norwegian-American serial killer who "loved her suitors to death" is believed to have killed many of the men she lured to her remote rural home in the late 1800s and early 1900s with promises of marriage via lonely-hearts newspaper ads stating "triflers need not apply." It's not known exactly how many victims the stout hog butcher ultimately claimed, usually by poisoning and robbing them. Gunness, played by Traci Lords in a 2021 movie, allegedly bludgeoned one suitor with a sausage grinder and buried another in a gunny sack on her farm, where more than a dozen sometimes dismembered and decapitated corpses were dug up from shallow graves. The "Black Widow" is rumored to have killed as many as 40 victims and faked her own death in a fire. Though the charred body of a headless woman was found on her property, some believe it was a plant and part of a pattern.

By some accounts, she originally purchased her farm outside La Porte with insurance proceeds after her confectionary business burned down. She had bought the confectionary with insurance money after her Chicago home burned down. The morbidly curious have long made pilgrimages to the gruesome

Belle Gunness continues to captivate the local imagination. There was once even a Lego display of the "husband killer" in the Lubeznik Center for the Arts in Michigan City that depicted her with an ax and skeletons buried under her farm.

The Shed when it was located on "K" St. in La Porte

Skull
Unknown Victim.
Found in the Privy on the
Gunness Farm.

BELLE GUNNESS EXHIBIT

WHAT: Serial killer exhibition at La Porte County Historical Society Museum

WHERE: 2405 Indiana Ave. #1, La Porte, IN

COST: $5 for adults

PRO TIP: The site where her now-razed farm once stood can be seen on McClung Road by Fishtrap Lake.

Left: *One of the most prolific serial killers of all time, Belle Gunness was also a skilled hog butcher.*

Right: *The skull of one of Belle Gunness's suitors rests in the La Porte County Historical Society Museum.*

mass burial site where courtship turned deadly. You can see an informative exhibit about "the Bluebeard in skirts" in the local history museum that includes her farm implements, a garden cart she used to haul bodies to her pigpen, and a shed that survived the blaze. The museum also features exhibits of vintage cars, antique weapons, and period rooms that show what life was like in town at different junctures. Many people visit just to learn more about Gunness's dark exploits. Notably, the skull of one of her victims lies under a glass case.

ECOLOGY'S BIRTHPLACE

Where was the field of ecology invented?

University of Chicago Professor Henry Chandler Cowles was reportedly so struck by the variety of the landscape as his train passed through the Indiana Dunes that he jumped out while it was still moving to get a closer look. In the early 1900s, Cowles would frequently bring his students to Northwest Indiana sites like Gibson Woods in Hammond and the Indiana Dunes National Park, which is today the fourth most biodiverse in the United States. Forged by the inexorable push of the Wisconsin glaciation more than 10,000 years ago, the landscape features dune grasses, globally rare oak and savannah trees, woods, marshes, and other ecosystems. Cowles, an Ecological Society of America founder who served as a field assistant for the US Geological Survey, studied the succession of vegetation from the sandy beaches to grass-draped dunes to oak forests. Many of his students went on to advance the practice of ecology in America, such as with the study of Mississippi floodplains and the development of the idea of biomes.

> ## COWLES BOG
>
> **WHAT:** Prehistoric bog named after ecology's founder
>
> **WHERE:** 1450 North Mineral Springs Road in Dune Acres, IN, with additional parking at the Greenbelt Lot at 1184 North Mineral Springs Road
>
> **COST:** Free
>
> **PRO TIP:** The nearby Calumet Trail that runs for miles under NIPSCO power lines also offers a good hike or bike ride where you can spot Great Blue Herons, wild turkeys, and other wildlife.

While Cowles conducted field research all across the dunes, you can see a full array of the biodiversity in Dune Acres at Cowles Bog, a 4,000-year-old wetland named in honor of the professor that was declared a National Natural Landmark in 1965. You trek past bogs, ponds, black oak savannas, forests,

The Cowles Bog bears the name of "father of ecology" Henry Chandler Cowles.

and tall reeds where birds alight. The varied landscape includes flowering water lilies, mossy logs, and a boardwalk that extends through the tree line. The 4.7-mile hike along the Cowles Bog Trail is no idle stroll with 202 feet of elevation up steep sand dunes. It pays off with a spectacular reveal of the beach and the endless expanse of Lake Michigan. A plaque honors Cowles near the trailhead, but nature's sweeping majesty pays even greater tribute than words cast in bronze ever could.

The sand at the Indiana Dunes is always shifting, allowing for continuous renewal. As plants die they provide a richer, more fertile soil for new species in what's called *succession*, which Henry Chandler Cowles studied in Northwest Indiana.

MOUNT BALDY

Where can you visit a sand dune that swallowed a boy and later a road?

Michigan City's Hoosier Slide was once the most popular tourist attraction in Indiana. But the towering mountain that people slid down was eventually strip-mined to make Ball-brand glass jars and foundations for Chicago buildings, railyards, and parks. Mount Baldy off Dunes Highway in Michigan City succeeded it as the tallest dune in La Porte County. The towering hill of sand stands about 126 feet high. Adventurous types have long clambered up to the summit to be able to see for miles around, all the way to the Chicago skyline on a clear day.

That ended when a boy was apparently swallowed down an 11-foot-deep shaft in 2013, likely to have been an air pocket created by a decayed, fungus-ridden black oak tree the dune had subsumed. The boy survived and even marched as the guest of honor in Michigan City's Fourth of July parade the following year, but it took his panicked family and onlookers three hours to dig him out.

The dune was closed to the public afterward, but people can still take National Park Service Ranger–guided tours and visit the adjoining beach by a power plant's hyperbolic cooling tower that has often drawn comparisons to Homer's workplace in *The Simpsons*. A wandering dune constantly on the move, the ever-shifting Mount Baldy moves four to ten feet a year as a result of the prevailing northwest winds and too many people trampling

At Mount Baldy Beach, you can go for a dip in Lake Michigan or sprawl out in the sun. During the offseason when it's less crowded with beachgoers, it's a great place for a long contemplative walk along the shoreline.

MOUNT BALDY

WHAT: A sand mountain that swallows everything in its path

WHERE: 101 Rice St., Michigan City, IN

COST: Free

PRO TIP: While in Michigan City, stop at one of the fine restaurants like Panini Panini, Muchos Mas, Royale with Cheese, or Shoreline Brewery.

Top: *Mount Baldy, once known as the Moon Dune, is so called because of the lack of vegetation.*

Inset: *Mount Baldy is slowly eating the parking lot.*

on the marram grass that stabilizes it. The living dune continues to migrate inward. In 2021, it started to swallow the exit road in the parking lot, which was already limited to about 90 spaces. While you technically still aren't allowed to climb the roaming hill, you can cross through a scenic wooded trail to the swimmable beach in its shadow. In addition, there are the "Singing Sands" that squeak underfoot and sweeping views of Lake Michigan.

TREE GRAVEYARDS

What's buried in tree graveyards?

The Indiana Dunes are living formations of sand, always roiled in motion like the crashing waves along the shore. Dunes have been known to move up to 60 feet a year. The constant shifting of sand contributes to the great biodiversity by seeding pioneer plants in new places and by killing other plants off by exposing their roots, allowing the mulch to nourish the soil in the cycle of life. One by product of the Indiana Dunes's ever-shifting sands is tree graveyards where thickets of dead trees jut out of the sand that left them stranded without any nourishing soil. Sand dunes have swallowed up entire forests. The phenomenon of tree graveyards can be found throughout the Indiana Dunes where it's not uncommon to see half of a tree's roots hanging out of a dune that's crept further landward. A few of the most dramatic spots include the Big Blowout by Trail 10 in the Indiana Dunes State Park, the terminus of the

GREAT MARSH TRAIL AT INDIANA DUNES NATIONAL PARK

WHAT: A great spot to see tree graveyards

WHERE: S Broadway Ave., Beverly Shores, IN

COST: Free

PRO TIP: Spend some time on the wooden observation deck surveying the marsh, as flocks of sandhill cranes often land and linger there.

Tree graveyards may look desolate but can be part of the broader ecosystem. The vast marsh filled with denuded tree trunks at the Highland Heron Rookery, for instance, appears ghostly from a distance but brims with birds.

Top: *Tree graveyards can be found throughout the Indiana Dunes.*

Inset: *The shifting sands of the Indiana Dunes leave many trees behind in soil that's too sandy and barren for them to thrive.*

Paul H. Douglas Trail in the Miller Woods in Gary's lakefront Miller neighborhood, and the Great Marsh Trail in Beverly Shores.

Even in areas otherwise teeming with wildflowers, reeds, ferns, forests, and other plant life, hikers can come across otherworldly assemblages of dead trees sticking out of the sand. On the beach, old pieces of driftwood add to the eeriness. It's a spooky, post-apocalyptic sight but one that emphasizes how fleeting life can be and how even the sturdiest-seeming oak is ultimately sapped of its vitality. The landscape of dried-out grey wood and bare, branchless tree trunks reaching up to nowhere as they slowly rot away can invite somber rumination about mortality and other weighty matters. But the trails continue to unfurl with varied plant life like colorful orchids and sweeping seas of prairie grass. And the nearby sun-bathed beaches beckon.

ROY BOY'S BADLANDS

What do tattoos, tigers, and rock stars have in common?

Roy Boy's Badlands in Gary was where celebrities like Lenny Kravitz, Cher, Steven Tyler, and Gregg Allman went to get inked. The original Tiger King, Roy Boy Cooper kept tigers that were eventually seized by federal agents in his notorious tattoo shop on Broadway in Gary. He's long dead, the tigers are in wildlife rescues, and rock stars are no longer making their way to rough-and-tumble Midtown Gary, but the tattoo ink keeps flowing.

Cooper was about as anti-authoritarian as it got, once painting "F-off" in six-foot-tall letters on the roof of the Bethlehem Steel mill and allegedly knocking a foreman's teeth out with a single punch. The weightlifter pumped iron in his seedy old-school establishment. An attitude-swollen sign for Roy Boy's Hardcore Gym read: "First off this is a gym, not a rehabilitation center or a baby daycare for crack users, beer drinkers, etc. So tell your hard-luck stories to your friends at home or the bars." Gary had a reputation as a rough place which the FBI deemed the "murder capital of the United States." Embracing this moniker, Roy Boy asserted, "We're No. 1 in murders and damn proud of it."

A staple in tattoo magazines in the 1990s, Roy Boy was especially known for the tigers that roamed his stores. The heavily tattooed bodybuilder loved his cats, which he took to exhibitions around the Region even after one bit his leg, leaving

A tiger is etched onto Roy Boy Cooper's tombstone, along with the inscription "3 can keep a secret if 2 are dead." A short documentary film, *Queen of the Badlands*, recently came out and can be watched on YouTube.

Don't be deterred by the door. Roy Boy's was once a nationally famous tattoo parlor.

ROY BOY'S TATTOOS

WHAT: A legendary tattoo parlor where tigers once roamed

WHERE: 3844 Broadway, Gary, IN

COST: Free

PRO TIP: Another rough-and-tumble tattoo place in Gary, Famous Legs Tattoos on Ridge Road, presents a photo op with an evil clown in the window and the humorous sign "our tattoos last longer than most marriages."

him with a permanent limp. In his heyday, he ran two parlors across the street from each other on either side of Broadway where bikers, rebels, and rule-breakers flocked to get tattooed or pierced at a time when a simple mention of the city of Gary invoked fear in many. His wife Debra, the "tattooed lady," continues to ink anyone bold enough to come in.

MARRIAGE MILL

Where did celebrities once go to get hitched?

Crown Point's Old Courthouse was once known as the Marriage Mill, churning out countless quickie Vegas-style weddings in the first half of the 20th century. At the time there was no wait and no requirements like a parent's permission or a blood test to wed in Crown Point. The only real rule was you couldn't be drunk. It drew couples from all over the country, including many famous people like Muhammad Ali, Harold "Red" Grange, Joe DiMaggio, Tom Mix, Ronald Reagan, and Rudolph Valentino, a silent film–era movie idol who tied the knot in Crown Point at the height of his celebrity. The dark-haired star, who rose from being a homeless immigrant to fame and fortune, often played the villain in the early days of Hollywood, starring in hits like *The Sheik* and *The Four Horsemen of the Apocalypse*. After divorcing his first wife, he embarked on a whirlwind romance with Natacha Rambova and married her in Mexico in 1922, only to be arrested for bigamy when he returned. It was then illegal to remarry within a year.

The couple visited Crown Point to wed the next year while staying in the Blackstone Hotel in Chicago. Then one of the biggest movie stars, Valentino circled the courthouse square twice after the wedding, greeting fans and signing autographs for hours for the assembled masses. The marriage only lasted two years, ending bitterly. Valentino later left Rambova only $1 in his will. The Old Courthouse, known as the Grand Old Lady, has regular Marriage Mill celebrations,

OLD LAKE COUNTY COURTHOUSE

WHAT: Site of historic Marriage Mill

WHERE: One Courthouse Square, Crown Point, IN

COST: Free

PRO TIP: Check out the Old Courthouse Shops, where you can find vinyl records at Antique Vault & Records, cooking supplies at Mescalore, or unique playthings at Toys in the Attic.

The Old Courthouse in downtown Crown Point, known fondly as the Grand Old Lady, was once the "Marriage Mill." It was a national destination for quickie weddings, drawing many celebrities over the years.

letting couples wed in the courtroom, under the rotunda, or on the steps outside. Built in 1878 with a dramatic mix of Romanesque and Gregorian architecture, it was nearly torn down and turned into a parking lot in the 1970s but was preserved and added to the National Register of Historic Places.

"The building is famous for more than being a marriage mill," Mark Skertic wrote in *A Native's Guide to Northwest Indiana*. He noted that populist presidential candidate William Jennings Bryan addressed thousands crowded around the square, a focal point for Crown Point's vibrant downtown, a regional destination for dining and antique shopping.

INDIANA DUNES

Where can someone find a rare flower that grows in Indiana only on the northern slope of one specific sand dune?

The Indiana Dunes, which sprawl across the Indiana Dunes National Park and the Indiana Dunes State Park along Lake Michigan's South Shore, are known for their beaches and Singing Sands that squeak underfoot. The sandy, sunny coastline has been called "a miracle of survival" because of how Dorothy Buell, Save the Dunes, and other preservationists rescued a portion of it from the encroachment of steel mills and other heavy industry. It's one of the most biodiverse places in the country because the shifting sands cause perpetual-motion-machine-like renewal of plant succession. The birthplace of American ecology, the dunes are home to more orchid species than Hawaii. The National Parks Service estimates that these dunes support up to 350 bird species and more than 1,100 types of flowering plants and ferns.

The dunes foster rare plants like the Fringed Polygala, a woodland herb colloquially known as Gaywings because its irregular petals spread like wings. The flower, which blooms either purple or white, is so rare that the only place it grows in Indiana is on the northern slope of one particular dune. Part of the genus Polygala that encompasses more than 500 species, Gaywings is so common in other Upper Midwestern states that it carpets some forest floors, but it is at the edge of its range in the Indiana Dunes. The distinctive flower is recognizable

---

The Indiana Dunes operates more than 25 different sites across 15 miles of lakeshore. Many are further inland and they're spread out, so plan accordingly.

The Indiana Dunes National Park stretches across 15 miles of Northwest Indiana's Lake Michigan lakeshore.

because of its fringed crest and lateral petals that spread far wider than the shorter and lower petals. Park rangers keep this endangered species' location secret, but photographers have managed to track it down and post pictures online. One can continue to explore the sandy expanses of the dunes to find a variety of plants like the Pitcher's Thistle, Rue Anemone, Large Flowered Trillium, Dutchman's Breeches, Smooth Solomon's Seal, Sand Cherry, Fringed Gentian, Tall Goldenrod, and Red Osier Dogwood.

INDIANA DUNES NATIONAL PARK

WHAT: One of the most biodiverse places in the country

WHERE: Addresses vary but the Welcome Center at 1050 N Mineral Springs Rd., Chesterton, IN, makes a good starting point.

COST: Free most places but $6 to get into West Beach.

PRO TIP: Seek out less visited places like Tolleston Dunes, Glenwood Dunes, Great Marsh, and the Heron Rookery, where herons no longer congregate but continue to fish in the Little Calumet River.

AN ARCHITECTURAL LANDMARK

Why did renowned architect Helmut Jahn design buildings in the Region?

Chicago-based German-American architect Helmut Jahn was widely regarded as a rock star in his field. He took his buildings to great heights that included One Liberty Place in Philadelphia, the Sony Center on the Potsdamer Platz in Berlin, and the Suvarnabhumi Airport in Bangkok. His legacy in Chicago includes the Joe and Rika Mansueto Library at the University of Chicago, several buildings in the Loop, a few buildings at O'Hare, and the endangered James R. Thompson Center, a cause célèbre among local preservationists. A stylish figure who landed a *GQ* magazine cover, Jahn received every major architectural accolade there was, including a major retrospective at the Chicago Architectural Center months after his death. Jahn, who died in a bicycle accident at the age of 81 in 2021, designed a few buildings in Northwest Indiana such as La Lumiere

Photographers have flocked from all over the country to photograph the Michigan City Public Library. The Art Institute of Chicago has even bussed students to the landmark for tours.

Top: *The courtyard offers a place for quiet rumination at the Michigan City Public Library.*

Inset: *Famed architect Helmut Jahn designed the downtown Michigan City Public Library.*

Gymnasium in La Porte and the De La Garza Career Center in East Chicago.

The 35,000-square-foot library he designed at 4th and Franklin streets in downtown Michigan City is considered a masterwork. It was one of his first projects in the 1970s when he was still employed by C.F. Murphy, which he would later buy and rename Jahn Architects. Cater Manny, a Michigan City native who worked for the firm at the time, landed Jahn one of his first public project commissions in the lakefront city. It was an instant landmark. The glassy building with a sawtooth roof won multiple construction awards, including one from each of the American Institute of Steel Construction and the American Institute of Architects. Library director Don Glossinger described it as a beautiful place to work. He noted that it still looks ultra-modern after 40 years, is flooded with natural light, and overlooks an immaculate courtyard centered around a Thomas Scarff sculpture. "It's a joy to be here," he told *The Times of Northwest Indiana.*

THE GREAT ESCAPE FROM THE BROWN MANSION

Why did a woman climb up a chimney and jump off the roof of a three-story mansion to elope with her motorcycle-riding boyfriend?

Loretta Brown escaped from her parents' Chesterton mansion with parkour-like maneuvers: scampering up the chimney, jumping off a balcony, and sliding off the roof to meet up with her waiting boyfriend, who was parked down the street on his motorcycle. She ended up marrying Valentine Cole after they roared off together in the dark of night to elope. Eventually, they moved back in with her parents, much to their chagrin.

Generations of the prominent Brown family lived in the grand three-story mansion that was built in 1885. Today the distinguished structure is owned by the Chesterton Public Library and managed by the Westchester Historical Society. It's home to the Westchester Township History Museum, which has artifacts like stereopticons, temperance pledges, and prehistoric mastodon bones dating back 10,000 years. It's a repository of information about the Duneland community, such as how it was settled by Irish immigrants, how its clay deposits made the

The Westchester Township History Museum boasts extensive archives, including memorabilia from the Prairie Club, the Richardson Wildlife Sanctuary, and the *Chesterton Tribune*'s photo collection. You can make appointments with the research department to access the materials.

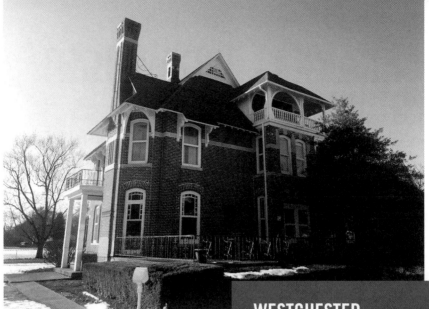

The prominent Brown family long resided in the mansion that's now home to Westchester Township History Museum.

WESTCHESTER TOWNSHIP HISTORY MUSEUM

WHAT: Local history museum in the Brown Mansion

WHERE: 700 W Porter Ave., Chesterton, IN

COST: Free

PRO TIP: Make sure to go on the highly informative guided tour.

town of Porter a hub for the brick industry, or how Chesterton's long-running Wizard of Oz Festival once drew fans of the movie from all over. The museum charts the sad history of how many of the sand hills in the Indiana Dunes were strip-mined for glass jars, foundations for Chicago buildings, and Northerly Island—formerly the Meigs Airport—that's now an outdoor concert venue. Tour guides are highly informative, regaling visitors with tales of Porter County history and bits of trivia. They know their stuff, including why Chesterton has so many Irish pubs or how preservationists finally succeeded in their decades-long campaign to save the dunes. The well-stocked gift shop carries more than 100 locally themed products from Indiana Dunes coasters to regional history books and local art. There you can view the juxtaposition of panoramic photos of townspeople posing in nearly identical positions while gathered in downtown Chesterton a century apart.

FRANK LLOYD WRIGHT HOMES

Where can you see Frank Lloyd Wright houses in Northwest Indiana?

Frank Lloyd Wright was one of the greatest architects of all time, at least if you give any credence to the American Institute of Architects and popular acclaim. Fallingwater, the Solomon R. Guggenheim Museum, the Johnson Wax Research Tower, and the Robie House are preeminent architectural icons that stand the test of time. The incredibly prolific architect of Usonian homes and other groundbreaking structures designed more than 1,000 buildings and completed more than 23,000 architectural drawings in his lifetime.

Some of his grandest blueprints never came to fruition, such as the mile-high Illinois skyscraper that would have dominated the Chicago skyline. Based in Chicago and Oak Park, the Prairie Style pioneer designed a few Northwest Indiana homes, including the Wilbur Wynant House in Gary that unfortunately was razed and reduced to an empty lot after a 2006 fire. Wright also designed the Ingwald Moe House in Gary and the Andrew Armstrong House in Ogden Dunes, which was named for an advertising director in Chicago, once visited unannounced by the founder of Domino's Pizza and sold for $1 million in 2021. Wright personally supervised

---

FRANK LLOYD WRIGHT HOUSES

WHAT: Works of a master architect

WHERE: 669 Van Buren St., Gary, IN, and 43 Cedar Trail, Ogden Dunes, IN

COST: Free

PRO TIP: The Frank Lloyd Wright House in Gary is located just a few blocks from the Cathedral of the Holy Angels, a spectacular religious structure that's worth a stop.

Top: *Frank Lloyd Wright designed a house on a dune in Ogden Dunes.*

Inset: *Only one of the two houses Wright designed in Gary still survives.*

the construction of what's also been called the Armstrong Dunes House. He praised the topography of the land that shaped his flowing design. Neither home hosts tours but you can admire them from the street. The homes are worth seeing as only about 300 of his buildings remain standing. Others can be visited nearby at the University of Chicago; South Bend; and Racine, Wisconsin. He designed three homes in St. Joseph and Benton Harbor, neighboring cities separated by the St. Joseph River just across the state line in Southwest Michigan. His son John Lloyd Wright, an architect who followed in his father's footsteps and took up residence in Long Beach, also designed many buildings across Northwest Indiana, many in the International Style.

After a decade's hiatus, the Armstrong House was the first residence that Frank Lloyd Wright designed in the Chicago metro area. It has many of his signature features, including obtuse angles, an organic multi-level layout, and a hidden entrance tucked behind the carport.

29

NIKE MISSILE BASES

Where can you play paintball in a former Nike nuclear missile silo?

Near Hobart, a Nike Missile Base was part of the last-ditch line of air defense for Chicago and the Region's steel mills during the Cold War, capable of shooting radar-guided supersonic missiles at incoming bombers with nuclear payloads. Now it's a paintball field that has occasionally doubled as a haunted house during the Halloween season. The Nike Missile Base C-47 in Hobart was one of 20 surrounding Chicago and one of 250 anti-aircraft batteries the Army built as part of the deterrence doctrine during the 1950s and 1960s as defensive rings around major cities and industrial centers. Built in the 1950s, the 20-acre base is one of just three listed on the National Register of Historic Places.

Blastcamp Paintball & Airsoft took over the historic missile base, incorporating 13 original buildings like radar towers and a fallout shelter into its playing field. Players can roam through barracks, the mess hall, and an administrative building, giving the paintball field an authentic military feel. You can see guard shacks, a shelter meant to shield soldiers from radioactive fallout, and military trucks that date back to the 1950s. The control center is separate from the launch site about a mile north, where the underground missile bunkers are located. After being decommissioned in 1972, it has hosted paintball matches for about 40 years and was also previously home to the annual Tour of Terror haunted house in which fright-seekers made their

---

The paintball camp took over the manned part of the base, but the missile launch site is located farther north at W 700 N in Hobart. It's fenced off, but the silos are supposed to be filled with long-stagnant rainwater anyway.

Left: *The old Cold War–era missile base is now a paintball field.*

Right: *Nike Missile Base C-47 stood ready to defend Chicago and Region steel mills from Soviet bombers.*

NIKE MISSILE BASES

WHAT: The former Nike Missile Base C-47, now Blastcamp Paintball & Airsoft, and the William S. Powers State Recreation Area

WHERE: Blastcamp is at 563 W 600 N, Hobart, IN, while the state park is at 12949 S Ave. O, Chicago, IL.

COST: $25 for Blastcamp, free for state park

PRO TIP: You can take part in walk-on play between 9 a.m. and 4 p.m. Also, look for Oozlefinch gear in the gift shop in honor of the mythological bird that air defense artillerymen adopted as a mascot.

way through a zombie infestation of the old military base. For anyone who takes an interest in Cold War history, there's also Nike Missile Sites in Porter and Wolf Lake, which spans Chicago and Hammond. At the William S. Powers State Recreational Area on the Illinois side of the border, you can see the display of one of the Nike-Hercules missiles that was supposed to shoot down incoming bombers if the Cold War ever heated up.

A COMMUNION WITH CRAFT BEER

What old church has craft beer on tap?

Beer Church in New Buffalo, Michigan, a popular Chicagoland summer getaway with steel mill–free beaches, repurposed an old Methodist Church that is now a craft brewery. Located just off Dunes Highway, it's so close to the beach you can see Lake Michigan from the parking lot. The brewpub is a must-visit when going to this beach town in Harbor Country just across the state line in Southwest Michigan. It's been featured in the *Chicago Tribune* and also described as "the Wrigley Field of brewery beer gardens" and "the single greatest beer garden mankind has ever contemplated." It specializes in small-batch beers, including India Pale Ales, sours, and a cream ale. A few beer names play up the religious theme like the Pontius Pilate double dry-hopped New England IPA. The food menu includes pizza that can be enjoyed al fresco in the expansive outdoor beer garden.

> ## BEER CHURCH
>
> **WHAT:** Okay, this one's pretty self-explanatory.
>
> **WHERE:** 24 S Whitaker St., New Buffalo, MI
>
> **COST:** Just the cost of a beer.
>
> **PRO TIP:** Consider sitting out on the sunny, spacious patio on a warm summer day and trying the "Communion Bread" (flatbread) appetizer.

The brewery in a church dating back to 1861 features a Vesuvio oven imported from Italy to bake Neapolitan pizzas. The wood-fired oven that the owners call "the Cadillac of ovens" was formed with clay from a mountain in Naples and is inscribed with the phrase "Chiesa Della Birra" (Church of Beer). Felix "Flex" Maldonado, who did the Jackson 5 mural on a four-story tower in downtown Gary and the Michael Jordan

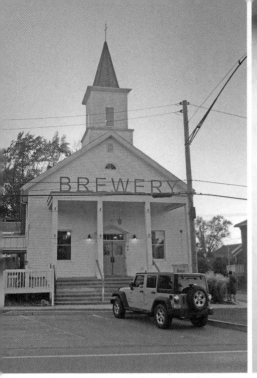

Left: *Chicago media have deemed Beer Church to be pilgrimage-worthy.*

Right: *In the future, everyone will have their 15 minutes of Beer Church.*

mural in East Chicago, crafted a mural entitled Graffiti Renaissance in the brewery dining room that's meant to evoke the Wynwood neighborhood in Miami that's been called a "living outdoor gallery." Once a year, the brewery does a special release of Midnight, a 17% ABV American Imperial Stout that's served in 16.9 ounce bottles. If you're in town, be sure to visit the Ghost Isle Brewery, the legendary Redemak's roadside burger joint, and of course the beach that put Harbor Country on the map.

Beer Church has fun with its religious roots. It encourages people to visit its "hallowed grounds," describes signing up for its email list as "joining the congregation," and vows it will offer free wifi "'til death do us part."

MEYER'S CASTLE

Why is a Scottish castle in Rust Belt Indiana?

Meyer's Castle, a staggeringly enormous 28-room estate modeled after a Scottish castle, sits anachronistically in Dyer, a bedroom suburb of Chicago. The medieval fortress just off US 30 was designed by locally prominent architect L. Cosbey Bernard Sr. for Joseph Ernest Meyer, one of Northwest Indiana's first millionaires. Meyer built his fortune as a horticulturist and herbalist who founded Indiana Botanic Gardens on the banks of the Little Calumet River in Hammond. Now the oldest retailer of herbs in the United States, the company sold medicinal plants via The Herbalist Almanac mail-order catalog to customers all over the world at a time when doctors were more scarce and self-treatment more common.

In 1929, Meyer commissioned the design of the Jacobethan castle based on one that impressed him on his travels. Built from Indiana limestone between 1927 and 1931, the regal residence boasts Tudor arches, Flemish gables, decorative chimneys, and 165 mostly casement windows. Surrounded by woods, it was one of the Region's most lavish homes. After Meyer died in 1950, his vast property was subdivided and developed into Castlewood subdivision. The elegant Meyer's Castle has been a long-running wedding and special events venue that can host up to 300 guests, though it was previously home to an Argentinian steakhouse. The place drips with

Joseph Meyer created an herb empire via mail-order catalog, and Indiana Botanic Gardens still operates in Hobart. It was located in a mansion at 636 177th Street in Hammond that's now home to Goodtimes Fireworks and the Reapers Realm Haunted House.

MEYER'S CASTLE

WHAT: A Scottish castle in unlikely environs

WHERE: 1370 Joliet St., Dyer, IN

COST: Free

PRO TIP: Take the time to stroll all around the expansive grounds. The ample gardens are filled with statues, fountains, and other unexpected sights to seek out and marvel at.

Top: *The Scottish castle in suburban Chicago is just as eccentric as you'd expect.*

Inset: *A peacock roams around the grounds of Meyer's Castle in Dyer.*

ambiance. Gargoyles loom over the front gate, which is flanked by elaborate wrought-iron street lamps. The winding road up the hill to the mansion looks as spooky as if it was drawn by Edward Gorey. The grounds are filled with wonders, such as a replica Venus De Milo and other classical sculptures, an alligator statue poking out of the tall grass, stone fountains, and an Easter Island head. An avid herbalist, Meyer planted many lush gardens on the sprawling, hilly, 11-acre property. Wander amid the carefully tended grounds, well-manicured lawns, and ivy-draped trellises. You might bump into a peacock strutting around.

35

ONE OF THE MOST SCENIC TRAILS IN AMERICA

Where can you hike on one of the most scenic trails in America?

USA Today named Trail No. 9 at the Indiana Dunes State Park the most scenic trail in America. High praise, and the trail doesn't disappoint. Once you ascend towering sand dunes to the peak of a dune ridge, there are breathtaking views of theendless expanse of Lake Michigan, the sweeping coastline, and sandy beaches to be savored. To the south, there's an equally endless sea of forest. A walk along the narrow ridgeline hundreds of feet in the air offers a panoramic view of a more isolated end of the Northwest Indiana shoreline. The trail winds around the edge of dunes circling the Beach House Blowout, a massive bowl of sand that frames the sandy landscape and vast lakefront in an epic way. The Hiking Project named it "the definite trail in the dunes." Park at the Nature Center, set off down the trailhead, and trek up Beach House Blowout ridgeline until Lake Michigan comes into view to be treated to a sumptuous visual feast. After some moderately strenuous uphill hiking,

---

TRAIL NO. 9 AT THE INDIANA DUNES STATE PARK

WHAT: One of the most scenic trails in the country

WHERE: Trailhead is near the Indiana Dunes State Park Nature Center at 1600 N 25 E, Chesterton, IN

COST: $7 for in-state, $12 for out-of-state

PRO TIP: Check out the Nature Center and traverse other trails, including the nearby 3 Dunes Challenge that lets you ascend three of the tallest dunes in the park: Mt. Jackson, Mt. Holden, and Mt. Tom.

USA Today *named Indiana Dunes State Park's Trail No. 9 one of the most scenic in the country.*

hikers are rewarded with the type of spectacular vista that will make one spontaneously whoop and pump one's fist in the air.

The trail progresses along the ridgeline with an elevated eagle's eye view of the Lake Michigan shoreline and also passes by the Furnessville Blowout before circling back around. A local hiker described Trail No. 9 as "perhaps the best trail in Northwest Indiana with incredible views of Lake Michigan." It's the crown jewel of the 2,182-acre state park at the north end of State Road 49 in Porter County that was established in 1925. It's often ranked as the most-visited state park in Indiana but it is locked in a perpetual rivalry with the fall foliage of the Brown County State Park for the top spot attendance-wise. Always bustling in the summer, the Indiana Dunes State Park features three miles of beaches, wetland, forest, and countless birding opportunities.

The trailhead is by the Nature Center, which is filled with exhibits about indigenous plants, bird migration, the fur trade history, and Lake Michigan shipwrecks. Check out the vintage South Shore Line posters and birds flitting around feeders out back.

OCTAVE CHANUTE, GRANDFATHER OF FLIGHT

Where did an innovator of flight first soar?

Carl Sandburg described the Indiana Dunes as "to the Midwest what the Grand Canyon is to Arizona and Yosemite is to California." The sweeping swathe of sand hills isn't just a natural wonder; it's also been a cauldron of creativity for artists, dreamers, and inventors. "Grandfather of flight" Octave Chanute inspired the Wright brothers with his hang glider experiments at the Indiana Dunes in Gary. The French-American engineer from Chicago who idolized Benjamin Franklin came up with the fixed-wing airplane concept that went on to dominate air travel. In 1896, he ran experiments with hang gliders on the Lake Michigan beaches, gathering extensive aerodynamic data from 700 successful flights after he and his assistants leaped off 75-foot-high dunes with gliders he designed. He shared his findings with Orville and Wilbur Wright, the bicycle shop–owning brothers from Dayton, Ohio, who built on his research to invent powered flight.

Though Wilbur Wright said after Chanute's death that "the history of flight would have been quite different had he not lived," the aeronautical pioneer never got wider recognition outside of the aviation world and the Region. He is celebrated

Octave Chanute, the first person the Wright brothers called after their successful test in Kitty Hawk, North Carolina, fashioned his pioneering Chanute glider out of spruce, using rattan and silk to make the wings.

Statues and plaques honor Chanute at the Gary Bathing Beach Aquatorium near where he conducted his flight experiments.

GARY BATHING BEACH AQUATORIUM

WHAT: Tribute to "Grandfather of flight" Octave Chanute

WHERE: 6918 Oak Ave., Gary, IN

COST: Free

PRO TIP: You can make a reservation to check out a replica of Chanute's 1896 camp on the Lake Michigan beach by calling 219-938-8080.

outside the Gary Bathing Beach Aquatorium in Miller, in the BP Innovators Hall of Fame in Hammond's Indiana Welcome Center, and on a mural outside his namesake Octave Grill in Chesterton. Outside Marquette Park's Aquatorium, a historic beach pavilion that was renovated to serve as a lakefront wedding venue, there's a plaque installed by the New York–based National Soaring Museum dedicated to Chanute's historic achievement, a life-sized bronze statue of him, and a replica of the glider he flew over Lake Michigan. Notably, his scarf rustles in the wind. Step out onto the beach with the winds whipping off Lake Michigan and it's not hard to figure out why Chanute chose to conduct his experiments there. Stroll along the shoreline and imagine gliders first taking flight.

THE FROST HOUSE, A TEMPLE OF 1960S STYLE

Where can you live a Mad Men lifestyle in Michigan City?

Forensic pathologist Dr. Robert and Amelia Frost lived for a half century in a rare prefabricated house in Michigan City that embodies the height of 1960s style. The 2,340-square-foot rectangular steel and glass home was one of fewer than 100 mass-produced modular homes made with baked enamel panels by the Akron, Ohio-based Alside Homes Corp. The now-defunct company that held patents on the unique design planned to make 200 a day but ended up going under like many firms attempting to revolutionize homebuilding with new materials or construction methods during the suburban boom of that era. The long, flat-roofed three-bedroom house was designed with geometric form by the esteemed architect Emil Tessin, evoking both the International Style of architecture and the Modern Movement. The distinctive dwelling dating back to

THE FROST HOUSE

WHAT: Retro architectural marvel

WHERE: 3215 Cleveland Ave., Michigan City, IN

COST: Free

PRO TIP: There's no on-street parking and Cleveland Avenue is a busy road, so you might need to park down the street if you plan to take photos.

The distinctive 1960s prefabricated home sits just across from Barker Woods, which is open to the public from dawn to dusk. It's one of the many natural areas preserved throughout Northwest Indiana by the Shirley Heinze Land Trust.

The Frost House is a mid-century modern marvel.

1958 is adorned with white, blue, and yellow aluminum panels that pop with color, giving it serious retro curb appeal.

Chicagoans Karen Valentine and Bob Coscarelli stumbled on the midcentury gem, dedicating themselves to its stewardship after buying the property a few miles south of Lake Michigan sight unseen in 2016. It came with the original Knoll furniture and interiors crafted by master furniture designer Paul McCobb. After moving in, they discovered it had been a sales model and was impeccably well-preserved. "It was like walking into a museum or time capsule," Coscarelli told Dwell, which named it the No. 1 prefab house in the country. It was featured in *Look Magazine* in the 1960s and ended up garnering a new round of media coverage after they chronicled its history on thefrosthouse.com website, documented it on an Instagram account that garnered thousands of followers, and got it listed on the National Register of Historic Places. It snagged coverage from Curbed Chicago and Crain's Chicago Business, which described it as a "time capsule of fashionable life in the 1960s" with "Mad Men cool." Only a dozen Alside homes remain and no others are in such mint condition.

The couple ended up selling the Frost House they bought for $192,000 for $850,000 after just a few years. Bids flowed in from as far as California when they decided to sell. New buyers who did not wish to be identified said they would continue to preserve the property but have not said if they would still host tours and other public events. You can still pop by outside and take pictures.

SS *EASTLAND* DISASTER

How is the deadliest Great Lakes disaster commemorated?

The SS *Eastland* was ferrying employees from Western Electric Company's Hawthorne Works in Chicago across Lake Michigan in 1915 to a picnic at the lakefront park in Michigan City when it capsized on the Chicago River, killing 884 crew and passengers. The boat was packed to capacity with 2,570 passengers when it started to tilt, lurched, and rolled over at the dock. Hundreds of people were trapped below deck in the capsized vessel, some crushed by pianos, bookcases, and other furniture as water filled the ship. It became a ghastly grave in which "picnic hampers, derby hats, and vacuum bottles bobbled alongside the bodies." The deadliest maritime disaster on the Great Lakes wiped out 22 entire families and killed 220 Czech immigrants, who comprised much of the company's workforce. The picnic was a big deal for the workers who were not granted much vacation at the time.

Future Chicago Bears coach and owner George Halas, then 20, was slated to be on the SS *Eastland* and was even listed as dead by newspapers but was unharmed because he didn't show up until after the ship had overturned. The sinking of the passenger steamship is commemorated outside the Old

---

MEMORIALS TO SS *EASTLAND* DISASTER

WHAT: Chicago Maritime Museum or Old Lighthouse Museum grounds

WHERE: 1200 W 35th St., Chicago or 1 Washington St., Michigan City, IN

COST: $10 for adults, $5 for students and seniors

PRO TIP: If checking out the Chicago Maritime Museum, be sure to carve out time for the art galleries in the Bridgeport Art Center. If you see the memorial at the Lighthouse Museum Washington Park, it's customary to snap some pictures of the city's landmark lighthouse.

Left: *A historic fountain outside the Old Lighthouse Museum quenches the thirst of "man, beast and bird."*

Above right: *An exhibit at the Old Lighthouse Museum highlights the SS* Eastland *disaster and other shipwrecks.*

Lighthouse Museum in Michigan City's Washington Park, a sprawling lakefront park that includes a beach, marina, zoo, restaurants, and other attractions. A memorial anchor chain was installed on the museum grounds in 2015 with every link representing one of the lives lost. The chain stretches 265 feet, as long as the *Eastland* that was renamed the USS *Wilmette* after it was converted into a US Navy gunboat following the disaster, in a sobering testament to the scope of the tragedy. An exhibit at the Chicago Maritime Museum on Bubbly Creek in Bridgeport also commemorates the lives lost on the improperly ballasted ship, including those who boarded and were never found.

The SS *Eastland* disaster proved one of the deadliest in Chicago history even though it happened in water that was only 20 feet deep just yards from shore, because many people were trampled while trying to escape or trapped below deck.

COMMUNITY VETERANS MEMORIAL, ONE OF NORTHWEST INDIANA'S SEVEN WONDERS

What war memorial features professional sports stadium-quality statuary?

Unlike most war memorials that are dedicated to a particular war, Community Veterans Memorial in Munster pays tribute to every modern war the United States has fought. It's a stroll through history complete with voiceover narration. The modern memorial has been described as "magnificent" and "one of the most interactive memorials in the country." Author Phyllis Thomas called it "realistic, sober and affecting." Voted one of the "Seven Wonders of Northwest Indiana" by *Times* readers, it was built at a cost of $3.2 million in 2003 and attracted more than 100,000 visitors from across the world in its first year.

The nine-acre tribute across the street from Centennial Park features separate memorials for each of the major wars in which the United States fought. It's populated by ultra-realistic bronze granite sculptures such as a Vietnam War grenadier, a Buddhist temple, and life-size monuments like a helicopter

COMMUNITY VETERANS MEMORIAL

WHAT: One of Northwest Indiana's Seven Wonders

WHERE: 9710 Calumet Ave., Munster, IN

COST: Free

PRO TIP: The world-renowned 3 Floyds brewery is a short distance away and it has a retail outlet where you can stock up on merch, comics, and of course the craft brewery's award-winning "not normal" ales.

Left: *Munster's Community Veterans Memorial remembers those who served in every 20th-century war.*

Right: *The sculptors who crafted the statuary at the Community Veterans Memorial also have pieces outside the United Center and Wrigley Field.*

landing outside a temple in Saigon. It's so scenic, gift cards of the various tableaux are available at the South Shore Arts Gift Shop. The sculptures were crafted by the married couple Julie and Omri Rotblatt-Amrany, who maintain a studio in nearby Highland Park, IL. She has taught at the Art Institute of Chicago and designed the 16-foot-tall Michael Jordan sculpture outside the United Center, while he did the 12-foot-tall Harry Caray statue outside Wrigley Field. They collaborated on Detroit Tigers statues at Comerica Park and on the sculptures at the Munster war memorial, many of which are quite poignant. There's a hollow man depicting the PTSD suffered by soldiers deployed during the War on Terror. It's a somber, contemplative space where you can ruminate on the horrors of war and the sacrifices young soldiers made. You can stop at stations along the trail and click a button to get fact-laden audio tracks about that particular conflict. Take time to listen to the voiceovers and engage in contemplative silence by the ponds to take in the full experience.

Veterans from Munster VFW Post 2697 lead guided tours between April 1st and mid-November. The tours are free of charge and tailored to fit the group.

FRANK DUDLEY'S DUNELAND

What landscapes inspired a legendary landscape painter to create his masterpieces?

Frank Dudley built his artistic reputation on his frequent paintings of the dunes and the rolling sand hills along the roiling Northwest Indiana lakeshore that inspired him so. He was drawn to the Indiana Dunes and became a major figure in their preservation from the encroachment of industry. Enamored after his first visit in 1911, he painted realistic landscapes of the wild and majestic dunes en plein air from sweeping vantage points, capturing the ever-shifting sand hills in different seasons, lights, and times of day. Dudley gave up his job running an art supply store to paint full-time in a log cabin studio in what's now the Indiana Dunes State Park in 1921.

"The Painter of the Dunes" aimed to bring the picturesque dunes indoors with naturalistic paintings like *The Land of Sky and Song* and *Under Changing Skies*. Despite a monomaniacal focus on the Region's shoreline to the exclusion of almost any other subject, he racked up a haul of accolades, including the Logan Medal of the Arts, the Young Fortnightly Prize, and the Art Institute of Chicago's Butler Prize. The landscapes he painted were often featured by the Hoosier Salon and mistaken for alien fantasy when exhibited at the Art Institute by museum goers

More than 100 cabins—including the governor's—were once at the dunes but were razed in the 1960s. The exact location where Dudley painted was never marked for posterity. It's believed to be a bluff overlooking the lake near Mount Holden.

Left: *Frank Dudley painted in a cabin at what is now the Indiana Dunes State Park.*

Above right: *Frank Dudley's work hangs at the Brauer Museum in Valparaiso.*

INDIANA DUNES STATE PARK

WHAT: Painter Frank Dudley's muse

WHERE: 1600 N 25 E, Chesterton, IN

COST: $7 for in-state, $12 for out-of-state

PRO TIP: It's worth trekking by the Works Progress Administration-era front gates to read the inscribed quotes, including one by poet John Milton celebrating the natural beauty that's abundant at the dunes.

who failed to realize such a rich environment was in their own backyard. Dudley's compositions helped lead to the establishment of the Indiana Dunes State Park in 1925 and the national park nearly a century later. He remained in a cottage owned by the state of Indiana until 1952 by donating a painting a year to that state. The cabin where he resided no longer exists, but you can hike far and wide across the dunes and soak in many of the same views he painted. You also can now view his artwork at the Indiana State Museum in Indianapolis, the Brauer Museum in Valparaiso, and many places across Northwest Indiana.

THE HOOSIER SLIDE

How does one slide down a sand dune?

The majestic Hoosier Slide in Michigan City was once Indiana's top tourist destination that drew visitors from far and wide, including many from Chicago. But the gently sloping 200-foot-tall sand dune people loved to slide down was hauled out a century ago and melted down to be made into glass for Ball Jars. Muncie industrialists hauled all the sand away to mass-produce the blue-tinted Mason jars that are now often found in antique stores. The giant, gently sloping dune could be seen from miles around, serving first as an early landmark for Native Americans and then later on for the French settlers. People started climbing it for the sweeping view of the lakefront. It wasn't long before thrill-seekers started sliding down the steep hill, picnicking at the summit, or getting married on what seemed to be the top of the world. It was a thriving

The Ball Brothers Glass Manufacturing Company in Muncie produced millions of blue Mason jars for years. The distinctive color came from the Hoosier Slide. By 1936, all 13.5 million tons of sand were exhausted, and Ball was only making clear jars.

Top: *A NIPSCO power plant stands at the site of the erstwhile Hoosier Slide.*

Inset: *A marker honors the Hoosier Slide outside the Old Lighthouse Museum in Michigan City.*

recreational destination by 1900, and was featured in most postcards depicting the Indiana Dunes during that time.

Muncie's Ball Corporation eventually started hauling away the heaping mound's sand, initially by the wheelbarrow, then the steam shovel, and finally the railcar. It took 30 years to remove all the sand, even at a clip of 30 train cars a day. It was ultimately reduced to nothing but a memory. The utility NIPSCO bought the site in the 1920s and built a massive coal-powered generating station there, a towering landmark often mistaken for a nuclear power plant because of its hyperbolic cooling tower that looks like Mr. Burns's power plant in *The Simpsons*. NIPSCO is now looking to raze the plant as part of a shift to renewable energy. A few places in town still pay tribute to the memory of the Hoosier Slide, including a towering woodcut by Corey Hagelberg at SFC Gallery in the Uptown Arts District and a plaque outside the Old Lighthouse Museum that remembers it as a "great tourism attraction."

THE SPARKLE HOUSE

Where can you see the sparkliest house there is?

The Sparkle House in Gary's Miller neighborhood is a passion project by artist Jennifer Taylor, a self-taught painter specializing in the strange and whimsical. She owns the Painted Board Studio gallery that started on Lake Street and is also an actor who's appeared in shows like *Empire* and *Chicago Fire*. No stranger to guerilla art projects, Taylor drew attention by hanging dresses in the long-abandoned Holiday Inn on Dunes Highway to highlight the scourge of abandoned buildings in Gary, helping lead to the ghastly motel frame's eventual demolition. She moved her artistic base to a long-abandoned, century-old house in Miller that she transformed into a sparkly source of inspiration that she hopes will "spark change" in a city that's long suffered from blight and vacancy.

Taylor, who has exhibited her work in venues like the Marshall J. Gardner Center for the Arts and Fluid Coffeebar, covered the ranch house in sparkles and transformed it into an art studio that hosts classes, visiting artists, and wine-and-painting evenings. It welcomes groups for art-making parties. She envisions the Sparkle House as an art project similar to The Heidelberg Project that transformed a dilapidated Detroit city block with eccentric artistic installations, salvaged items, and bright polka dots. Just eight minutes from the beach, the Sparkle House can be rented out on Airbnb. Those staying get free use of all the art supplies in the studio to create their own

The Sparkle House is rented out as an Airbnb. You can stay in a unique home that's close to the beach and Miller's art galleries while getting free access to the owner's art-making supplies.

The Sparkle House is building out a labyrinthine sculpture garden.

SPARKLE HOUSE

WHAT: Shiny, sparkly art house

WHERE: 6128 E 6th Pl., Gary, IN

COST: Free

PRO TIP: It's easy to pull over on the shoulder of the road to snap pictures but be wary of passing vehicles.

paintings and are helping to fund the labyrinthine sculpture garden she's building out in the front yard. The house itself is a work of art and visitors often snap pictures of it while visiting Gary's lakefront Miller neighborhood, a bohemian enclave filled with art galleries, unique restaurants, and natural areas like the Miller Woods, Miller Lagoon, and Marquette Park along the Lake Michigan shoreline.

SOUTHERNMOST POINT OF LAKE MICHIGAN

How far south does one of the greatest of the Great Lakes go?

You can swing by Gary's Marquette Park to see the southernmost point of Lake Michigan, the only Great Lake that falls entirely within the borders of the United States. A marker depicting the big blue lake recognizes the geographic point on the far south shore of the third largest Great Lake by volume and the fifth largest lake in the world. You can't miss it; there's a sign by the road that directs you to its location. Lake Michigan creates the South Shore that's home to the Indiana Dunes National Park, the Indiana Dunes State Park, and many other beaches. Northwest Indiana is in fact sometimes marketed as the South Shore, such as by the South Shore Convention and Visitors Authority and Gary SouthShore RailCats. It's like an inland ocean with no end in sight.

Local civic boosters George Rogge and Sue Rutsen, who spearheaded the Aquatorium preservation, the Nelson Algren Museum and Pocket Park, and many other community initiatives in Miller, spearheaded the effort to install the geographic marker on the beach. It makes for a great photo op and a unique point of interest. The educational sign informs visitors that 3,500 ships and planes lie at the lake's

MARQUETTE PARK

WHAT: Site of southernmost point of Lake Michigan sign

WHERE: 1 N Grand Blvd., Gary, IN

COST: Free

PRO TIP: Stop by the nearby Miller Lagoon for some great photo ops. If you drive south on Lake Street and stop on the bridge, you can capture a dramatic view of the lagoon while smoke billows from the Gary Works steel mill off in the distance.

Lake Michigan is the largest body of water in the United States.

bottom and that the Great Lakes contains a fifth of the freshwater in the entire world. It also explains how vital Lake Michigan is as a source of drinking water, international transportation, and recreation. Marquette Park is also filled with many other interpretative historical signs, explaining how this was a place where Octave Chanute conducted flight experiments, Nelson Algren gained inspiration for his books as he walked through these woods, and how the course of the Grand Calumet River was reversed for industry creating the Miller Lagoon. It's like an outdoor museum. You can stroll around and learn a lot about local history.

Lake Michigan is named after the Ojibwa Indian word Mishigami, which means "large lake." People from outside the area are often surprised to see how large and oceanic Lake Michigan actually looks from the shore.

CACTI IN INDIANA

Where can you go to see a cactus in Midwestern Indiana?

No one expects to see a cactus in Indiana, the land of endless flatness and rows of corn stretching off into the horizon. It almost sounds like a joke. Iowa-based hipster T-shirt chain retailer Raygun in fact sells a postcard at its Chicago store with a towering cactus that says "Greetings from Indiana: We Save on Postcard Expenses by Purchasing Stock Photos of Arizona." But the Indiana Dunes—a sweeping desert of rolling sand hills preserved by both the Indiana Dunes National Park and the Indiana Dunes State Park—hosts an almost incredible array of biodiversity, where you can see pine trees sharing space with cacti. Cacti are prevalent in the desert-like sands of the duneland and almost impossible to miss when hiking in the Miller Woods or the trails at West Beach in the Indiana Dunes National Park. They're low-lying, often shorter than tufts of wild dunegrass, and nearly impossible to kill, as many Miller Beach residents in Gary can attest. The best time to see them is in June and July when they start to flower, displaying what's been described as "showy yellow blossoms."

A great place to see the prickly pear cacti is in the John Merle Coulter Nature Preserve in Portage on the Gary border. The 94-acre state-dedicated nature preserve is named after former Indiana University President and University of Chicago

Not the outdoorsy type? You can still see clusters of the prickly pear cacti outside the Depot Museum and Art Gallery in Beverly Shores. The Beglin Native Plants Garden across the street showcases an impressive variety of flora and fauna.

Yes, cacti grow in Indiana.

JOHN MERLE COULTER NATURE PRESERVE

WHAT: Good spot to see cacti in the wild

WHERE: Northeast of County Line Rd. and US 12/US 20, Portage, IN

COST: Free

PRO TIP: Bring bug spray, watch for snakes, and stay on the trail, which leads to a fragile blowout dune. The nearby Depot Dog hot dog joint in an old train depot is definitely worth a stop.

Botany Department Chair John Merle Coulter, who taught Henry Chandler Cowles, the professor who invented the field of ecology while studying biodiversity and plant succession in the Indiana Dunes. A nearly mile-long trail winds through the park by the MonoSol plant, where you can see more than 400 species of plants like wildflowers and showy ferns amid the prairie, oak savanna, and wetlands. You can take in marsh marigolds, wild geraniums, and starflowers as well. Just keep an eye on the trail for racerunner lizards or hognose snakes underfoot while hiking.

CITY WEST, THE NEW CHICAGO THAT COULD HAVE BEEN

What happened where city rivaling Chicago was once envisioned?

Chicago once had a rival across the lake in Indiana. In the early 1800s, the Windy City had only about 200 residents along the southwestern shore of Lake Michigan. The rival City West sprouted about 60 miles away in what is now the Indiana Dunes State Park in Chesterton. The "dream city" was sketched out on a plat map that imagined a big town that was never realized. Developers only built a few buildings, including a sawmill, a tavern, and a hotel that provided lodging for travelers between Chicago and Detroit. Settlers gathered there despite the lack of a school or church, leaving children to idle, watching boats on Lake Michigan or harvesting wild berries.

The ever-shifting sand dunes swallowed up the cemetery that buried the local dead. The Great Depression swept across the land, leaving City West a ghost town filled with ruins, including houses that were ultimately subsumed by the wandering sands. City West burned down in a forest fire in 1853, nearly 20 years before Chicago rebuilt after the Great Chicago Fire. As with Ozymandias's vast and

CITY WEST

WHAT: Ghost town near the beachfront Dunes Pavilion at the Indiana Dunes State Park

WHERE: 1600 N 25 E, Chesterton, IN

COST: $7 for in-state, $12 for out-of-state

PRO TIP: Not far from the Dunes Pavilion stands a birding platform that gives you a panoramic view of the beaches along the coastline. Birders have spotted countless migratory species there, recording their findings on a big tracking board.

The Dunes Pavilion stands where the City West ghost town was planned.

trunkless legs of stone, all that remains to mark the grand city that was envisioned is the City West Park Shelter at the Indiana Dunes State Park. You can get a small sample of what could have been in the more than 90-year-old Dunes Pavilion at the site of the city that never was. The Art Deco beachfront pavilion recently underwent a $5 million renovation transforming a glorified storage shed into a hub of hospitality that hosts diners, wedding receptions, and people looking to indulge in a libation while watching the sunset over Lake Michigan with the Chicago skyline glimmering off in the distance. There's a general store, Dari Dip ice cream parlor, and two restaurants with outdoor balcony seating, offering a "million-dollar view of Lake Michigan and the beach."

Before Hollywood took over the movie industry, the South Shore dunes were often a stand-in for Egypt and the Sahara Desert during the early days of filmmaking. The stretch of coastal Indiana, most amenable to swimming during July and August, is easily accessible via highway and the South Shore Railroad.

MOUNT TRASHMORE AND THE LOST MARSH

Why do wedding parties pose for photos on a former dumpsite?

Heavily industrialized Northwest Indiana has a way of turning old waste sites into recreational treasures. A steel mill waste processing plant was transformed into the Indiana Dunes National Park's Portage Lakefront and Riverwalk. It's got a wedding pavilion, a fishing pier, the Burns Waterway boardwalk, and a location that's ideal for bird-watching and seeing shelf ice on Lake Michigan in the winter. Hammond's 18-hole Lost Marsh Course was built on a 70-foot-tall mountain of steel slag in what the EPA hailed as "the most successful brownfield reclamation project in the Midwest." A tony Frank Lloyd Wright–inspired clubhouse with a waterfall in the stairwell, an extensive wine collection, and a restaurant balcony patio overlooking George Lake now sits atop what was an unsightly heap of slag from local steel mills.

Though the rolling green fairways look bucolic, the industrial setting is inescapable with golfers on the driving range teeing off against a backdrop of mammoth oil tanks from a neighboring

---

Centennial Park was originally a brick factory and its lake a clay pit. National Brick in Munster supplied bricks to Chicago buildings for 80 years. The clay reserves were so tapped out when it came time to cap the landfill that clay had to be sent back from Chicago. It largely came from under the Museum of Science and Industry when it excavated an underground parking garage.

Left: *Lost Marsh Golf Course was built on a steel slag heap.*

Right: *The lake at Centennial Park was originally a clay pit.*

TRASH-TO-TREASURE PARKS

WHAT: Centennial Park and Lost Marsh Golf Course

WHERE: Calumet Ave. and N Centennial Dr., Munster, IN; 1001 129th St., Hammond, IN

COST: Free

PRO TIP: Don't miss the botanic gardens at Centennial Park and be sure to climb the hill for a view of the Chicago skyline on a clear day.

refinery. Another old dumpsite was turned into one of Northwest Indiana's nicest parks. With its sparkling waterfront, Munster's well-manicured Centennial Park is so aesthetically appealing one would never guess its history as a landfill. The towering trash pile was turned into a sod-covered hill known locally as Mount Trashmore. Crossfit classes sprint up there, couples embrace on the porch swings, and children rush up for the pristine first snow so they can rocket down on sleds. If you climb the fitness stairs, you can take in views of the Chicago skyline on a clear day. Centennial Park features formal gardens, a dog park, an amphitheater, a sculpture-lined trail, and a golf course. Indiana University Geologist Ken Schoon noted both dumpsites now have golf because it's one of the few sports where it doesn't matter if the ground isn't level as the waste decomposes underneath. Centennial Park's focal centerpiece is a lake with jetting fountains. Ducks, Canadian geese, and other waterfowl flock to the water, as do gaggles of groomsmen and bridesmaids posing for wedding photos in the summer. Don't miss the steel sculpture that asks, "What mark will you make upon the world?"

59

THE JINGLE JOHNS

Why are port-a-potties singing Christmas tunes?

Talk about toilet humor. One of the Region's weirdest holiday traditions animates brightly lit port-a-potties that sing Christmas carols and sometimes rap. Gary's Service Sanitation came up with an incredibly novel idea a few years back of synchronizing a port-a-potty light show to Christmas music. The firm supplies portable bathrooms to Lollapalooza, the Chicago Marathon, the Indianapolis 500, and nearly every construction site in the Region. It made its distinctively blue mobile restrooms the stars of unlikely music videos set to Trans-Siberian Orchestra, Snoop Dogg, and a mélange of musicians.

Marketing Manager Stevie "Dee" Dykstra came up with the idea of the humorous videos in lieu of traditional Christmas cards for customers and created a viral sensation by synching 100 port-a-potties to Straight No Chaser's irreverent a cappella classic The Christmas Can-Can. The singing toilets dubbed the Jingle Johns have secured wide-reaching media coverage from across the country, including from National Geographic, WGN, and Windy City Live. The Jingle Johns—A Lighted Loo Experience videos, which take countless hours to synchronize, have gotten increasingly elaborate over the years, featuring audio samples from *National Lampoon's Christmas Vacation* and a lip sync battle version of "Santa Claus is Coming to Town." A new video drops on YouTube every year, typically after Thanksgiving. It's almost always even more creative than the previous year's.

THE JINGLE JOHNS

WHAT: Caroling port-a-potties

WHERE: www.youtube.com/user/ServiceSanitation or www.servicesanitation.com/jinglejohns

COST: Free

PRO TIP: Check out one of the live shows, such as at the entrance of the Lincoln Park Zoo where you can also see the popular Zoo Lights holiday display.

The Jingle Johns go caroling throughout greater Chicagoland every Christmas season. Photo courtesy of Service Sanitation.

You can also catch Porta Paul, Carl Can, Buddy Blue, and Linda Loo performing a live show. The Jingle Johns choir also gets rolled out at local festivals, parades, and places like Zoo Lights at the Lincoln Park Zoo. It's choreographed to perform a medley of classic Christmas carols and modern hits at events like the Cedar Lake Parade and the Mistletoe on Main Street in Portage. There's a new act to see every year, and the Jingle Johns are always taking requests to make appearances.

Jingle Johns' songs are often topical, including a rendition of "Go, Cubs, Go" after the 2016 World Series and a "Hallelujah" chorus to celebrate the end of the pandemic-marred 2020.

BURN 'EM BREWING'S CREAMED CORN BEER

How does beer taste like canned corn?

Burn 'Em Brewing brews many unique beers, including one made with the unlikely but very Hoosier ingredient of creamed corn. The acclaimed craft brewery has a taproom in Michigan City and the Bare Bones Gastropub in downtown La Porte, which also offers a creative spin on pub cuisine such as a French onion grilled cheese sandwich. Its often unorthodox and sometimes experimental beers are crafted with unusual ingredients like graham crackers and toast coconut. They are distributed across Indiana and often come in 16-ounce tallboy cans that feature elaborate, panoramic comic book–esque labels and the slogan "Comforting the Distributed. Disturbing the Comfortable."

Burn 'Em's Kreamed Corn Cream Ale is brewed with actual creamed corn but isn't as saccharine as one would think. While creamed corn may sound off-putting in a beer, it makes for an easy-going brew. One reviewer on RateBeer, where it's ranked as "very good," described it as "bizarre but pleasant" and would "definitely recommend it to anybody who is up for something that is different and tasty." Though Kreamed Corn goes down smoothly, it's hardly sessionable at 6.2% ABV so watch how many you imbibe. It sports an American Gothic–inspired label where a pitchfork-toting skeleton and anthropomorphic corn

---

Michigan City also is home to Shoreline Brewery, the Brewery Lodge and Supper Club, and Zorn Brew Works, a historic brewery that closed during Prohibition and was revived as a craft brewery in the 21st century.

Left: *Burn 'Em Brewery is known for its creative beers.*

Right: *Okay, so this is corny.*

of cob share a pint while the rural countryside burns behind them. Burn 'Em is a staple at local liquor stores and on supermarket shelves, but it's so creative and offbeat it's still definitely worth a trip to the mothership to get it fresh from the source. Michigan City taproom offers al fresco seating under strung-up lights by a blueberry farm though plans were underway as of publication

BURN 'EM BREWING

WHAT: Home of creamed corn beer

WHERE: 718 Freyer Rd., Michigan City, IN

COST: Free

PRO TIP: The Yellow Pickled Egg at Burn 'Em is a far cry from the nasty, curdling snack in a jar one might expect at a dive bar. It is pickled with turmeric, Daikon radish, and carrot drizzled with both horsey and Thai chili sauce.

time to move it to a more highly-trafficked location on Dunes Highway. Burn 'Em serves up many highly original, out-there beers like the rosemary-based sour saison Beta Vulgaris, the Dark Side of the Moo chocolate milk stout made with cocoa nibs and lactose, and the Blueberry Mr. Tea bale brewed with both green and black tea leaves and fermented with blueberries grown just down the street.

THE REGION GOES TO THE MOVIES

Why did Napoleon Dynamite go bowling in the Region?

Many Hollywood movies have been filmed at least in part in the Calumet Region, where the Indiana Dunes often stood in for the Sahara Desert when Chicago was still a hub of the movie industry during the silent film era. *The Fugitive* filmed scenes in Whiting. Much of Johnny Depp's *Public Enemies* was shot in John Dillinger's old stomping grounds of Crown Point. Keanu Reeves's thriller *Chain Reaction* blew up the Inland steel mill (on-screen only). *Transformers 3*, *A Nightmare on Elm Street*, and *Original Gangsters* all were shot in abandoned buildings in Gary. The iconic Smiley Face water towers in Calumet City made an appearance in Oliver Stone's *Natural Born Killers*. And gosh, one film was shot almost entirely in Lansing. Actor Jon Heder and *Parks and Recreation*'s Jim O'Heir, a Lansing native, filmed *When Jeff Tried to Save the World* for weeks in the old-school Lan-Oak Lanes bowling alley on Ridge Road just across the state line. Heder, of course, is famous for playing Napoleon Dynamite in the cult classic that explores (among other things) high school alienation, Uncle Rico's delusions of football grandeur, and amazing nunchuck skills.

LAN-OAK LANES

WHAT: Where *Napolean Dynamite*'s star shot an indie film

WHERE: 2524 Ridge Rd., Lansing, IL

COST: $1.75 a game

PRO TIP: Watch the career of Munster native Kendall Goldberg, who's made several short films. *When Jeff Tried to Save the World* started out as a short film she was able to expand into a full-length feature.

Gosh, Napoleon Dynamite himself once filmed a movie at Lan-Oak Lanes.

A Munster native directed the indie film about a bowling alley employee who tries to save his beloved workplace from sale and demolition. It evokes underdog stories like *Rocky* while subverting expectations and providing an intimate character study into Heder's stunted protagonist who's settled into a cozy cocoon of warm complacency. He must first "pull himself out of the gutter" before he can save his beloved Winky's World. You can still roll at the throwback Lan-Oak Lanes, where the ambiance is thick and the history runs even deeper. While shiny new bowling alleys like Up Your Alley have since opened, the 16-lane bowling alley that's retained a 1960s look remains a classic place to play a few frames in a nostalgic environment.

Bowling is a cherished pastime in the blue-collar Region. Almost every city and town has an alley, Calumet College in Whiting competes for national titles, and bowling scores still appear in local newspapers.

STRADDLING THE ILLINOIS-INDIANA STATE LINE

Where can you stand with one foot in Indiana and one foot in Illinois?

It ain't exactly the Four Corners Monument in the Southwest but the Calumet Region is often called Illiana for a reason. While political grandstanding has made the boundary seem more pronounced in recent years, the Calumet Region stretches across state lines. Defined by the watersheds of the Calumet River, the Grand Calumet River, and the Little Calumet River, the Calumet Region stretches from the far South Side of Chicago through the south suburbs and Northwest Indiana all the way to Southwest Michigan. You can straddle two states in many places such as on the beach on Michiana Shores, along State Line Road at the border of Hammond and Calumet City, or on the trail outside Franciscan Hospital in Dyer. Two of the more interesting spots to stand (or boat) in two states are in Wolf Lake that's half in Indiana and half in Illinois and at the Illinois-Indiana State Line Boundary Marker, a historic obelisk by Hammond's former State Line Generating Plant site that forever marks that demarcation. The stone monument was built by the US Office of the Surveyor in 1838, is one of Chicago's oldest extant structures, and continues to demarcate the boundary between the two states

Wolf Lake on the Hammond side has an extensive boardwalk that lets you walk at water level over the gently rippling lake. You can get a good view of Great Blue Herons and majestic egrets fishing near the shore.

I'm in Indiana. I'm in Illinois. I'm at the Illinois-Indiana State Line Boundary Marker.

though it was moved about 191 feet along the border in 1988.

The adjoining area along the border of Hammond and Chicago makes for an interesting trek along the Lake Michigan shore. You can visit a secluded beach in Hammond west of the far more popular Whihala Beach in neighboring Whiting, just east of the lakefront Calumet Park on Chicago's Southeast Side, and next to the Hammond Bird Sanctuary that was previously known as the Migrant Trap. Hundreds of migratory bird species have been spotted at the 9.5-acre enclave of wooded lakefront that Audubon has described as "one of the most important flyways for migratory songbirds in the United States." It's most active during the spring and fall migrations.

ILLINOIS-INDIANA STATE LINE BOUNDARY MARKER

WHAT: Where you can stand with a foot in each state

WHERE: East end of Avenue G by Chicago or 100 Digital Crossroad Dr., Hammond, IN, which is accessible via the Hammond Marina

COST: Free

PRO TIP: Don't miss the nearby Hammond Bird Sanctuary, a wooded area that's been identified as one of the best places in the Calumet Region for identifying migrating passerines.

67

GARY DEMON HOUSE

Where can you find a portal directly to hell?

In Gary, allegedly. The Steel City was once home to the infamous Demon House, according to a 2014 *Indianapolis Star* story that captivated a national readership. Latoya Ammons claimed she witnessed many supernatural occurrences after moving into the home in 2011. She told authorities her children were possessed by demons, levitated, and walked backwards up the wall. The family brought in Michael L. Maginot, the priest from St. Stephen, Martyr Catholic Church in Merrillville to perform several exorcisms before they fled, moving to Indianapolis. This reputedly haunted house in Gary's Glen Park neighborhood was billed as a direct portal to hell. It attracted so many curious gawkers when the article first came out that the Gary Police Department had to dispatch extra patrols to the neighborhood in response to frequent complaints from neighbors about all the activity. Police also yanked the case report from public access after getting flooded with too many requests for it.

The home was later purchased for $35,000 by reality television star and paranormal investigator Zak Bagans, who used it as the site for a documentary called Demon House that drew comparisons to horror films like *The Exorcist* and *The Amityville Horror*. The tagline was "view at your own risk." Bagans "even started to wonder if just viewing the film could open audiences up to possession themselves— had he made a movie too dangerous to release?" He tore the

DEMON HOUSE

WHAT: Purportedly haunted house where Zak Bagans filmed a documentary

WHERE: 3860 Carolina St., Gary, IN

COST: Free

PRO TIP: There's not a lot to see today at the site, which is now an empty lot, so it helps to watch the documentary and read all the articles to best appreciate it.

Zak Bagans razed the Gary Demon House after shooting a documentary there.

house down in 2016, claiming it was just too evil, in what may have been an inspired stroke of marketing. The exorcist said that people still visit this unholy site of demonic possession, sometimes seeking to perform Satanic rituals. Today, the Demon House that's now featured in *Ripley's Believe It or Not* is just an empty grassy lot with a gnarled tree standing guard. Suspend your disbelief and soak in the spooky atmosphere.

The Region is filled with many supposedly haunted places, including the Inn at Aberdeen in Valparaiso, Kahler Middle School in Dyer, the Gypsy Graveyard in Crown Point, and the Stallbohm Barn-Kaske House in Munster.

HIGHLAND HERON ROOKERY

Where can you go to see Northwest Indiana's pterodactyl?

Seagulls flock everywhere in Northwest Indiana, from the beaches that stretch along the Lake Michigan shore to the asphalt seas of big-box-store parking lots and multiplexes. But the Region's official bird is the Great Blue Heron, which has been described as the pterodactyl of Northwest Indiana because of its great flapping wings, long sharp bill, and crested head. They're impressive, majestic birds that stand up to four feet tall. Famed bird guidebook author David Allen Sibley wrote that "they may appear graceful and elegant at a distance but up close the large size and dagger-like bill of the Great Blue Heron make it a fearsome predator." They're pretty and pretty hardcore. Check out the YouTube video where a heron in Florida swallows a baby gator whole.

Herons flock to the Little Calumet River, which is so shallow in places it has been described by a naturalist as "McDonald's for raptors." The stately herons can be viewed throughout most of the year at the Highland Heron Rookery, a nature preserve by LaPorte Avenue and Liable Road in Highland, just east of Homestead Park on the Little Calumet River that provides a convenient access point. Great horned owls also nest there.

Other great spots for viewing Great Blue Herons in Northwest Indiana include the Heron Rookery Trail near Michigan City, the Little Calumet River Trail near Porter, and the Calumet Trail in Porter County.

Herons, great horned owls, and countless other birds flock to the Highland Heron Rookery.

HIGHLAND HERON ROOKERY

WHAT: Habitat for Great Blue Herons

WHERE: W 7th Ave., Highland, IN

COST: Free

PRO TIP: Park at the neighboring Homestead Park in Highland and walk along the Little Calumet River Levee Trail for your best chance to see Great Blue Herons and Great Egrets wading in the shallow stretch of river hunting for fish.

An entire Audubon Field Guide's worth of birds flit about among the reeds and dead trees in the marsh south of the river, where Canadian geese, ducks, swans, and other waterfowl flock. Binoculars and benches along the trail provide spotting aids and resting places to birders. Photographers often gather there with high-powered lenses on tripods. A cacophony of chirping rains down from the treetops and white-tail deer sprint through the woods, but the star attraction remains the herons that wade near the shallow shoreline in search of fish. Downtown Hobart's Lake George is also a reliable place to see herons. Just head to the bridge over the Deep River Dam to watch them wading in search of seafood.

CITY AS CANVAS: GRAFFITI ART IN GARY

Which graffiti murals have received world renown?

Gary, a steel town that's been in decline for decades, has long been covered in graffiti, at first because of crime, urban blight, and depopulation. It's estimated that the city has had as many as 10,000 buildings that homeowners and businesses just abandoned, creating many opportunities for graffiti writers to leave tags or paint bigger, more artistically ambitious murals. In recent years, it's been splashed with commissioned, vibrantly colorful murals as a result of art projects like Lauren Pachecho's #PaintGary and Lake Effekt in the bohemian Miller neighborhood. The Decay Devils, a group of historians and photographers who seek to preserve landmarks, estimate that 85 different public art projects have been done in the city. Both downtown Gary and the lakefront Miller Beach community serve as outdoor galleries. Many of the notable murals are clustered downtown, such as those along the Indiana Toll Road, at Gateway Park, and on the multistory parking garage behind the Centier Bank Tower.

You can find a complete map online to track down the pieces. Most of the Lake Effekt murals can be seen by strolling along the Lake Street downtown commercial district and by poking

---

GRAFFITI ART IN GARY

WHAT: An urban playground for muralists

WHERE: The commissioned graffiti displays are especially concentrated downtown and in the Miller neighborhood. You can find a list and map in the Gary Public Art Archive + Guide at www.destinationgary.com or decaydevils.org/artguide.

COST: Free

PRO TIP: Bring a camera and plan your trip so there's plenty of good light for photographing some of the most striking murals.

The #PaintGary project covered the Steel City in colorful murals.

around in back alleyways and behind buildings. The project brings in new artists to freshen up the art by painting new works every two years, and you can watch them in action. Prominent artists like Ish Muhammad, Felix "Flex" Maldonado, and Ishmael Nieves of the famed Crazy Indiana Style Artists (CISA), an East Chicago collective that hung out with Keith Haring when he was commissioned to do work in Chicago. Internationally known artists like Hebru Brantley have taken part in Lake Effekt. It's one of many ongoing activities of the Miller Beach Arts and Creative District, which has sought to use the arts to energize the lakefront neighborhood that's lined with galleries and has long attracted en plein air painters and other artists.

Spectators can watch artists paint murals at either the Lake Effekt festival or the Arts on the Ave Festival in Hammond. The outdoor festivals feature craft beer, live music, and food from local restaurants like Flamingo Pizza.

PURDUE NORTHWEST SCULPTURE PARKS

Where can you play Frisbee golf in the shadow of a towering French tricycle?

Purdue Northwest used to consist of Purdue Calumet in Hammond and Purdue North Central in Westville. The two branch campuses sat about 45 minutes apart but were eventually merged in 2016 to form the state's fifth largest university. The commuter campuses share the Odyssey Sculpture Collection that populates the grounds with more than 40 contemporary sculptures. Launched in 1998, the program is named after a sculpture of Odysseus journeying for more than 20 years from the Trojan War back to his wife in Ithaca. It's a metaphor for how college students are charting their life courses. The often large-scale sculptures are valued at more than $6 million.

The contemporary pieces range from whimsical depictions of Segways and Victorian girls in billowing dresses to more sobering subject matter like a slave ship or the September 11 terrorist attacks. They're often set against dramatic backdrops. Tony Hendricks's *Tres Bon Tricycle* plonks a tower-size old-timey trike in front of a vast, open field flanked by a striking tree line in Westville. A solitary boatman paddles across a pond by

It's easy to miss some of the pieces in the extensive sculpture collection at the Purdue University Northwest Campus in Westville. Don't forget to look along US-421, by the basketball courts on the south end of campus, and near the access road off West County Road 125 South.

Left: *Tony Hendricks's* Tres Bon Tricycle *can be seen on the Purdue University Northwest campus in Westville.*

Right: *You can see sculptures on land and sea at Purdue University Northwest.*

PURDUE UNIVERSITY NORTHWEST ODYSSEY SCULPTURE AND ART EXHIBIT

WHAT: Contemporary sculpture walks on on the PNW campuses

WHERE: 2200 169th St., Hammond, IN, or 1401 US-421, Westville, IN

COST: Free

PRO TIP: If visiting the Hammond campus to see pieces like the Chicago sculptor John Adduci's abstract *Major*, be sure to stop by the library to see the exhibits and the permanent collection that lines the walls.

Shakespeare's Garden on the north end of campus like the ferryman Phlegyas crossing the River Styx, in one particularly dramatic photo opportunity as both the silver sculpture and the green tree line reflect a perfect mirror image across the still surface of the water. Bill Barrett's massive *Lexeme* was chiseled from marble from the same Italian quarry Michelangelo tapped for his masterpiece *David*. The campus also features public chess tables, colorful beach chairs, and a Frisbee golf course. While playing a round or just on a self-guided walking tour, one is inclined to roam all around the campus to make sure none of the stunning artworks go unnoticed. The Hammond campus also invites strolling to discover striking sculptures like herons and a solitary Sisyphus-like figure dragging chains. Columnist Philip Potempa described it as an "art adventure."

75

BRINCKA CROSS GARDENS

Where can you find a hidden garden cultivated by an Art Institute professor for 40 years?

Art Institute of Chicago Professor Bill Brincka and his partner Basil Cross devoted more than 40 years to cultivating a stunning garden behind their Frank Lloyd Wright–inspired home in duneland in Porter County. They nurtured four acres of impeccably landscaped gardens behind their architecturally distinguished home. Their property also encompasses 21 acres of pristine woodlands that are crisscrossed with trails. South Shore Arts Executive Director John Cain described it as "a masterpiece" where their "creativity can be seen throughout the gardens." After following a wooded trail back to the house, you discover the garden that blossoms forth with a stunning wealth of flora and fauna, including weeping trees. While wandering the well-tended grounds, you can see 450 varieties of daffodils, 400 types of hostas, 40 different ornamental grasses, and 25 types of crabapple trees.

BRINCKA CROSS GARDENS

WHAT: A secret garden

WHERE: 427 Furness Rd., Michigan City, IN

COST: Free

PRO TIP: Avoid trampling the flowers if you're there to take pictures.

Thousands of daffodils, magnolias, and forsythias bloom at the Brincka Cross Gardens every spring. The Porter County Parks Department has even started offering a Daffodil Hike guided tour.

Top: *A Frank Lloyd Wright–inspired house welcomes visitors to the Brincka Cross Gardens.*

Inset: *An Art Institute professor and his partner cultivated the Brincka Cross Gardens for decades.*

After Brincka (2001) and Cross (2006) passed away, their private residence and superbly cultivated gardens were acquired by Porter County Parks and Recreation, which turned the unique property into a public park. You can book a tour online or take a self-guided tour of the gardens and woodland trails. Horticulturist Matt Brown has helped to restore the founders' vision by tending to overgrowth and invasive species. The Brincka Cross Gardens have become a draw for photographers and a destination for weddings, corporate retreats, and special events. Porter County Parks and Recreation acquired a neighboring 36 acres with the intention of expanding the park, extending the trails, and restoring natural habitats for plants, birds, and wildlife. It's a place of quiet serenity that invites contemplation. Taylor Bundren, the public relations coordinator for Porter County Parks, described the park to *The Times of Northwest Indiana* as a "very calming, artistic place with a peaceful and calming atmosphere" that "just has a calming feel."

TAXIDERMY MOUNTAIN AT CABELA'S

How do elephants, polar bears, sea turtles, and a waterfall co-exist inside a suburban store?

Cabela's in Hammond is a Taj Mahal for outdoorsmen—a shrine to fishing, hunting, and camping. The gargantuan 185,000-square-foot destination big-box store just off the Borman Expressway wows with shock and awe the moment you walk in. A prop plane hangs overhead. A man-made mountain looms off in the distance. It's populated by museum-quality taxidermy animals like those found in Chicago's Field Museum, including polar and grizzly bears, pronghorn sheep, rams, mountain goats, and bobcats. The two-story mega-store is filled with taxidermy throughout, including a dramatic scene of wolves hunting water buffalo against the backdrop of a Bob Ross–like mountain mural by the cash register. Full-scale displays are nestled amid the sea of flannel shirts, fishing lures, and other merchandise. There's a section dedicated only to deer and another that features African lions, zebras, cape buffalos, and a full-sized elephant. Educational panels describe various species and what hunters have done for conservation.

The outdoor adventure superstore also boasts an aquarium filled with fish one can find in nearby Lake Michigan, as well as

Downtown Griffith's American Natural Resources is also another destination for taxidermy, which it has done on commission for nature centers, universities, and the Smithsonian. The sprawling shop showcases taxidermied black bears, big fish, and many raccoons prying into Cracker Jack boxes.

Left: *An elephant lords over the Africa wildlife diorama at the Cabela's in Hammond.*

Right: *A sea turtle hangs out in the aquarium at Cabela's.*

CABELA'S

WHAT: A Taj Mahal for outdoorsmen

WHERE: 7700 Cabela Dr., Hammond, IN

COST: Free

PRO TIP: Behind the big-box store in Hammond is a length of trail that tunnels under the massive Borman Expressway, which makes for an otherworldly stroll if you're so inclined.

a massive sea turtle. Everything about the Cabela's is over-the-top, such as the old-timey general store area that sells old-fashioned candy, hot sauce, and venison jerky. You can grab a game sandwich at the in-store restaurant or try out the bows in the indoor archery range. The sister Bass Pro Shops in Portage has similar attractions, including a mountain with a waterfall, bears, and an aquarium. A nearby display of a pack of wolves taking down an elk while another escapes brings to mind the joke about how you don't have to outrun the bear, just your slowest friend. If you're into the outdoors, you could easily spend a few hours just wandering around the aisles of either store. Think IKEA for a frame of reference of the size.

ARTESIAN WELL

How can you sample mineral water from a little-known aquifer spring?

Chicagoland has more lead water lines than anywhere in the world, an estimated 70,000 lines that could potentially poison tap water. So it's no surprise that Gary residents flock to a natural artesian spring in the Black Oak neighborhood to tap into unfiltered water from the earth. For decades, residents in the city's Black Oak and Small Farms areas have lined up to fill various containers with water that bubbles up naturally from an aquifer at a well off 35th Avenue and Chase Street. The unfiltered H2O allegedly contains minerals and medicinal properties. The well was more popular before Black Oak got municipal water during the 1980s but retains appeal for nostalgic natives. Just one of 15 artesian wells in the Hoosier State, it's the only one in Northwest Indiana.

"I used to bring my brother to get water. He's been drinking it for years," Alma Wilkes, 66, told the *Gary Post-Tribune*. "Every time we come, someone stops by and they have a story about it. I would think that if we see someone every time we come, it's still being used." If you're adventurous enough to try it, brace yourself for a strong mineral taste as the water is unfiltered. Old-timers advise letting it settle for a day, saying it then tastes a little sweet. It's cold out of the well, flowing nonstop from a crude spigot fashioned from a PVC pipe in a concrete block.

The Little Calumet River Basin Development Commission is planning many site improvements to the well location. Watch out for a small drive-in area with a lamp-lit four-space parking lot, a small park, and new piping for easier access.

Well, actually.

It's nestled amid the shrubbery off the side of the road at the southeast of the intersection and can be tricky to find the first time, but if you stick around the area for long enough cars will probably pull up there to help you pinpoint the location.

ARTESIAN WELL

WHAT: One of the few wells in Indiana

WHERE: Southwest of 35th Ave. and Chase St., Gary, IN, by the railroad sign

COST: Free

PRO TIP: Look for the railroad sign on the southwest side of the intersection at 35th Avenue and Chase Street. If you see a bunch of empty water bottles scattered around, you're in the right place.

THE GRANDE POLLUTION OF THE GRAND CALUMET RIVER

Which was once one of the most polluted rivers in the world?

As with the Chicago River, the flow of the Grand Calumet River was reversed to serve the needs of industry. The Grand Cal as it's known in the Region flows through north Lake County, running by steel mills, oil refineries, and some of the most industrialized land on earth. Named after the native word for peace pipe, the Grand Calumet River has carried toxic effluent for decades. As much as 90 percent of the flow of the river has consisted of industrial and municipal effluent. About 100,000 pounds of lead and 67,000 pounds of chromium once sat in the sediment at the bottom. It was notorious for being so polluted that even sludge worms that feed off toxins couldn't survive in such an inhospitable environment. Signs still warn people not to swim or fish there. Much of the fish population was wiped out during the 20th century. But after dredging and other remediation efforts, the watershed is again home to species like the Karner Blue Butterfly and the Black-crowned Night Heron.

GRAND CALUMET RIVER

WHAT: One of the most polluted rivers in the United States

WHERE: The headwaters can be viewed at the Miller Lagoon, which is accessible via a hike from Marquette Park at 1 N Grand Blvd., Gary, IN, or the Miller Woods at 75 Lake St., Gary, IN

COST: Free

PRO TIP: You have to hike through the Miller Woods to get to the river's headwaters. Keep an eye out for wildlife like beavers, turtles, and the birds that flit about on the reeds.

The Grand Calumet River is unsafe for swimming or fishing.

The river can be viewed from various points in Hammond, East Chicago, and Gary, including from the Calumet River Trail and Peoples Park just north of downtown Hammond and also from its headwaters at Marquette Park in Gary's Miller Beach neighborhood. One of the best places to see the river's natural splendor before it becomes adulterated by steel mill discharges is at the Miller Lagoon that was formed when the river was reversed. There are a few excellent viewing points, including from the Miller Woods, from Patterson Island which can be reached by Shinto-inspired walking bridges, and from the Marquette Park Pavilion. The Prairie Style special events venue that was built in 1924 is a local architectural landmark that features twin turrets, porte-cochere arches, and terraced balconies adorned with decorative flower pots. A sweeping stairway leads right up to the still waters of the lagoon, which is often covered by lily pads.

The Grand Calumet and Little Calumet Rivers were sections of the Grand Konomick River before they were channelized to serve industrial development. Cleanup efforts have long been underway to restore native species like bald eagles and make the rivers safe for activities like paddling.

FORD HANGAR IN LANSING

Why did one of the world's most famous industrialists build a pioneering hangar near the state line during the early days of aviation?

In 1926, the industrialist Henry Ford built the Ford Hangar on a 1,400-acre site in 1926 in Lansing. It was originally intended to be a manufacturing plant for the Ford Trimotor Airplane and to fly parts from Detroit to the nearby Ford Assembly Plant in Hegewisch. The Tin Goose was the first all-metal commercial airliner with multiple engines. Distinguished architect Albert Kahn designed the building so it would have large windows that let in natural light, sliding doors on a single rail that could be operated by one person, and a cantilevered lack of structural support that created a large open space that made it easier to move airplanes in and out. It was visited by Amelia Earhart, Jimmy Doolittle, Billy Mitchell, and Ford himself to promote aviation during the 1920s. The Great Depression grounded Ford's dreams of flight. Despite acclaim, only about 200 Trimotors were ever built. They still sometimes visit the hangar, and Lansing village officials have tried to acquire one to enhance the historic attraction.

The site is now home to the 600-acre Lansing Municipal Airport where planes take off and land more than 60,000 times

---

The historic Ford Hangar often hosts the popular Fetching Market. Artisans from across the country sell handmade wares, vintage finds, small-batch products, boutique clothes, and retro furniture. There's live music, local cuisine, and "delish cocktails."

Ford built a historic hangar at the Lansing Municipal Airport.

FORD HANGAR

WHAT: A historic airplane hangar built by Henry Ford

WHERE: Lansing Municipal Airport, 3250 Bob Markas Dr., Lansing, IL

COST: Free

PRO TIP: Lynnie Ques Barbecue at the Lansing Airport is a great place to eat ribs, drink beers, and watch planes land and take off. It's hidden away, accessible only by an elevator.

a year. It's where British Open champion "Champagne" Tony Lema was headed when his plane crashed on the seventh hole of a nearby golf course, tragically killing him and three others in 1966. The vintage Ford Hanger, which was placed on the National Registry of Historic Places in 1985, can be observed at the northwest corner of the municipal airport. There's an informative historical marker on the southwest side of the hangar, near the runway where you can watch planes land and take off. It's near the Lansing Veterans Memorial which features a statue of a soldier carrying a wounded battle buddy on his shoulder to an actual Vietnam-era Huey helicopter. Renowned actor Gary Sinise, who played Lieutenant Dan in the acclaimed film, *Forrest Gump*, once visited to raise funds for the memorial's preservation.

NELSON ALGREN POCKET PARK

Where did one of Northwest Indiana's most torrid love affairs transpire?

Novelist Nelson Algren was a bard of the down-and-out, a voice for the woebegone and wasted. He's known for chronicling the seedy underbelly of Chicago that he described as "like loving a woman with a broken nose—never a lovely so real." But Algren spent a lot of time in Miller, where he bought a lake house with the proceeds of his National Book Award–winning tale, *The Man with the Golden Arm*, which was made into a movie with Frank Sinatra. While going to grab a six-pack, he once slipped through the ice into the Miller Lagoon, where he almost certainly would have frozen to death if teenagers passing by hadn't pulled him out of the frozen waters.

French essayist Simone de Beauvoir was a groundbreaking philosopher and feminist icon. After a transatlantic correspondence, she and Algren consummated a love affair at his cottage in Gary's lakefront Miller neighborhood, where the Nelson Algren Trail was named in his honor in 1950. De Beauvoir visited him in Miller after an exchange of love letters. They reportedly sometimes made love atop the crest of a dune after paddling

Left: *Novelist Nelson Algren is immortalized on the side of the liquor store he once frequented.*

Right: *The Algren Trail follows the path along the Miller Lagoon the author often trekked.*

across the lagoon. At the time, Algren was one of the best-known and most celebrated literary writers in America.

Today, Algren is celebrated in Miller with a museum and the Nelson Algren Alley and Pocket Park located near one of his favorite local Miller establishments, Lake Street Liquors. A billboard-sized black-and-white photo of him now graces the side of the liquor store he once frequented. The alley is filled with pictures and quotes from Algren's work as well as a little free library with many of his books. There's also a Nelson Algren 606 Sound Stage just down Lake Street that hosts live music, author appearances, and other museum programs. It's tucked between the 18th Street Brewpub and Thumbs Up, where they serve half pitchers if you're really broke and down on your luck like an Algren character.

The Nelson Algren Museum in Miller, which is open by appointment only, houses his books, including *A Walk on the Wild Side*, and artifacts like his typewriter and a replica of the bike he used to pedal around Wicker Park.

ECOLOGY'S BIRTHPLACE (page 12)

PINHOOK BOG IN INDIANA DUNES NATIONAL PARK (page 158)

OCTAVE CHANUTE, GRANDFATHER OF FLIGHT (page 38)

FLORIDA TROPICAL HOUSE (page 132)

PULLMAN NATIONAL MONUMENT (page 182)

INDIANA DUNES (page 22)

RENSSELAER ART WALK (page 106)

CACTI IN INDIANA (page 54)

THE RUINS OF LONG-ABANDONED STEEL MILLS (page 152)

BARKER MANSION BLACKOUT TOUR (page 120)

HOOSIER VALLEY RAILROAD MUSEUM (page 178)

NATHAN MANILOW SCULPTURE PARK (page 150)

ST. ANDREW THE APOSTLE CHURCH IN CALUMET CITY (page 172)

RENSSELAER ART WALK

Why was a small town transformed into an outdoor art gallery?

The Rensselaer Art Walk has attracted praise and visitors from far and wide. The town is the county seat of the largely rural Jasper County and was long home to St. Joseph College. The downtown still has some life like the stalwart Ritz Theater, the farm-to-table Fenwick Farms brewpub, and the trendy Station at Embers restaurant. As with many small towns across the country, commerce moved out to chains along the highway, leaving downtown something of a ghost town. A public art campaign eventually put Rensselaer on the map again. Muralists from all over the country convened to give downtown Rensselaer a new coat of paint.

The RenArtWalk turned the historic commercial district into an outdoor art gallery where you can spend an entire afternoon walking around and taking photographs. Critics said the change is nothing short of amazing. Massive murals—some a few stories tall—depict Red Ibises, women in Japanese robes, and other dramatic scenes, including the phrase "You are loved" set against the backdrop of a heart on the wall of a bank branch. One can see dozens of murals while walking around downtown, which stretches only a few blocks. RenArtWalk was intended to foster a "creative environment that would enrich creative minds." The large-scale spray-painted murals are ultra-contemporary and hip but also family-friendly, featuring subjects

One can view an online gallery of the murals at www.renartwlk.org. But it's no substitute for seeing the scale of the work in person and stumbling across stunning art pieces in unexpected places.

The Rensselaer Art Walk is an outdoor art gallery.

RENARTWALK

WHAT: An outdoor art gallery

WHERE: Downtown Rensselaer

COST: 115 W Washington St., Rensselaer, IN

PRO TIP: Stop by Centennial Park downtown to see a few pieces along the embankment of the creek, including the placemaking *Rensselaer, Indiana* underscored like a felt baseball banner.

like bunnies, owls, turtles, cats, fish, and Ford Mustangs. The RenArtWalk includes many selfie opportunities, such as with butterfly wings splayed out like the now-iconic Los Angeles angel and the 3D umbrella which shields the poser from multi-colored rain. Find a map online and take a stroll through downtown Rensselaer to see all the distinctive art, including works from artists like Cameron Moberg, Emily Ding, Andres "Cobre" Iglesias, Chris Changyang Shim, and Jenna Morello. Make sure to poke your head down every alley if you don't want to miss anything.

CITY METHODIST CHURCH

How long has one of the most infamous urban ruins in the Midwest been abandoned?

Nearly a century ago, immigrants erected the immense City Methodist Church in downtown Gary, a towering testament to the Steel City's storied past. The visually dramatic Gothic church that reaches to the heavens has been featured in a Transformers movie, the *Nightmare on Elm Street* remake, and *Sense 6* by the Wachowski Sisters. Skilled craftsmen carved the looming nine-story cathedral in a hardscrabble steel mill town in 1925, seeking to civilize a rough company town populated with taverns, shanties, brothels, and hardened steelworkers who risked life and limb to forge the hardest metal of all. The Gothic church's fate was sealed almost from the start. It was dubbed "Seaman's folly" because Pastor William Seaman incurred the then-astronomical cost of $1 million to build a church that was way too big for the fledgling mill town. It was home to the largest Methodist congregation in the Midwest for decades before the Steel City suffered from heavy job and population losses along with increased crime.

The cathedral was turned over to Indiana University Northwest after its members dispersed to outlying suburbs

CITY METHODIST CHURCH

WHAT: Epic ruins of a towering Gothic cathedral

WHERE: 577 W Washington St., Gary, IN

COST: Free

PRO TIP: While many urban explorers and photographers break into the abandoned building, particularly to capture the first snowfall of the year, be mindful that the roof could collapse.

City Methodist Church may not be godforsaken but it was definitely forsaken by man.

but ended up being abandoned by IU in the 1970s. City Methodist Church stayed vacant for decades, a testament to how far the grand aspirations that compelled the City of the Century's founding had gone off course. The church suffered catastrophic fire damage after the Great Gary Arson of 1997. The sanctuary roof collapsed in 2014 while a news crew from Indianapolis was filming inside. A historic marker was recently installed outside. Gary has had plans to turn it into the country's largest European-style ruins garden. Despite its decrepit condition, the church continues to attract urban explorers from all over, including Europeans who often visit both Gary and Detroit. It's especially popular with photographers who seek to capture its eerie abandoned beauty after the first pristine snow there during the winter.

Gary has a wealth of abandoned architecture to see and photograph, including the Palace Theater; Union Station; the Old Post Office; and the Heat, Light & Water Building. The Decay Devils and others lead architectural tours.

WALL OF CRAP AT SCREAMING MONKEY COMICS

How can you read about the adventures of Kool-Aid Man and Hamster Vice?

Screaming Monkey Comics in Munster displays the *Wall of Crap*, a collection of the weirdest and saddest comic books they could find. The eccentric comic book store on Ridge Road near the Illinois border exhibits "embarrassing comics that should never have come to be" including *Alf*, *Superman Meets the Motorsports Champions*, *New Kids on the Block*, *Fish Shticks*, *Itchy Planet*, and *NFL SuperPro*—guest-starring Spider-Man, which was allegedly created so a comic book artist could get free tickets to the Super Bowl. The brainchild of a comic book artist and an advertising professional in Chicago, the shop ran in a barely visible spot in downtown Crown Point between 2002 and 2008, before the Great Recession killed its first run. The death proved to be as final as that of Superman or, really, any other comic book character. Owners John and Christina Yeo revived the store in Munster in 2019, where it built a following because of its wide array of graphic novels, value packs featuring complete story arcs, collectibles, board games, art classes, adult coloring books, and game nights with *Dungeons*

Northwest Indiana has many cool comic book shops, including Creative Comics, Happy Day Comics, Dragon's Lair, Heroes Haven, Monroe's Collectibles, and Galactic Greg's. Tenth Planet has a life-sized statue of Silver Surfer in the window that's worth checking out.

Screaming Monkey Comics is home to the Wall of Crap.

SCREAMING MONKEY COMICS

WHAT: Home of the *Wall of Crap*

WHERE: 21 Ridge Rd., Munster, IN

COST: Free

PRO TIP: The comic shop has value packs containing old editions of various titles and regularly hosts gaming nights and other events.

and Dragons and *Magic: The Gathering*. In keeping with its name, the store is filled with a number of monkeys, including stuffed animals and Gorilla Grodd action figures.

A highlight is the ever-expanding *Wall of Crap*, where you can marvel at the exploits of *Chuck Norris: Karate Kommandos*, a cynical tie-in with a *Mortal Kombat*–inspired cartoon that somehow featured art from the legendary Steve Ditko or a bizarre *Honeymooners* comic in which Ralph teams up with Captain Lou Albano in the wrestling ring to try to raise $1,000 to build a playground. The captions the store provides are about as snarky as you would expect and a delight to read. None of the misbegotten comics are for sale. "It's kind of like a museum piece," John Yeo said.

GIANT HOBO OUTSIDE RUBEN'S RESTAURANT

Where can you enjoy a hot dog by a 20-foot-tall hobo or in a mostly abandoned shopping mall?

Next door to the world's encased-meat capital, Northwest Indiana is home to many hot dog joints that specialize in Chicago dogs like Arman's, Koney King, Andy's Red Hots, or Arnie's, "where man bites dog." Two local hot dog joints are particularly unusual. Ruben's Restaurant in Lake Station is known for the giant statue of a hobo with a fistful of balloons, a bindle, a pocketful of linked sausages, and a shoe coming apart at the seams. Ruben's serves traditional Chicago fare like Maxwell Street Polishes, Italian beef, pizza puffs, and gyros. Its giant top-hatted hobo has made the place an unmissable local landmark. The mustachioed vagabond has greeted visitors to Lake Station since about 1960 and was once featured in a national calendar. High winds toppled the hobo in 2015, but it was restored even though the original manufacturer has long since gone out of business.

A few exits away on the Borman Expressway, Chuck Wheeler's cooks Chicago dogs in the largely abandoned Village Mall in Gary. The movie theater, Chinese restaurant, and

RUBEN'S RESTAURANT OR CHUCK WHEELER'S VIENNA BEEF

WHAT: Where to grab a hot dog under a giant hobo statue or in a nearly abandoned mall

WHERE: Ruben's is at 2230 Ripley St., Lake Station, IN. Chuck Wheeler's is at 3514 Village Ct., Gary, IN

COST: The price of a hot dog

PRO TIP: Go to Chuck Wheeler's for the hot dog, stay to tour the eerie, empty mall. The Village is mostly vacant and surreal to walk around, amid the ghosts of storefronts that once bustled with long-bygone shoppers.

A hobo traipses around outside Ruben's in Lake Station.

department store are all gone. But people still come to visit a mostly empty shopping mall just because the hot dogs are so good at an institution that's been around since the 1950s. Enshrined in the Vienna Beef Hall of Fame, it's best known for its Chicago-style hot dogs that have the twist of a unique pickled green tomato. It was founded by the late Charles Wheeler, who started out selling tamales from a scooter outside of taverns and won the Kentucky Fried Chicken franchise for Northwest Indiana after meeting with Colonel Harlan Sanders himself. He sold all 13 of his KFC restaurants and founded the Christ Community Church in Hobart after entering the seminary to become a pastor in the 1980s but remains a legendary name in Region fast food.

Green Fields just across the street from Ruben's Restaurant also is in the giant fiberglass statue game. The head shop has a giant elephant and rhino prowling along the Ripley Street corridor just off the Borman Expressway.

SURFING BY AN OIL REFINERY

Where can you surf by the largest oil refinery in the inland United States?

People surf in Indiana, believe it or not. As Ted McClelland noted in *The Third Coast*, "surfing in Indiana sounds as ludicrous as a cattle drive across Delaware" and "Northern Indiana is not a surf-movie backdrop with its steel mills, foundries, and gray pennants of smoke, with Chicago's skyscrapers looming off in the distance." But surfers ride some serious waves in Lake Michigan. No Hawaii, Venice Beach, or even the "Malibu of the Midwest" Sheboygan, Wisconsin, the south end of Lake Michigan is mainly a winter surfing spot. The waves can be choppy the rest of the year, but the winter generates swells big enough to catch and ride. When winds blow south, Lake Michigan—which is more than 300 miles north-to-south—can generate tall, powerful waves that break cleanly, especially when old industrial shipping piers or breakwaters block the crosswinds. When a passerby questions whether the waves get big enough for surfing in *The Third Coast*, a surfer points out, "Hey, the *Edmund Fitzgerald* went down in twenty-foot waters."

Surfers must wear full-body wetsuits and have a certain amount of wild, devil-may-care abandon. They brave bitter cold, chilly water, icy slush, and sometimes gale-force winds on Lake

Lake Michigan gets polluted periodically. The Surfrider Foundation sued steelmakers along the lakefront over hexavalent chromium releases in the hope of cleaning up the lake for recreational activity. Surfers have expressed concerns about rashes, infections, and kidney problems.

People do surf on Lake Michigan.

WHIHALA BEACH

WHAT: Popular spot to surf by an oil refinery

WHERE: 1561 Park Rd., Whiting, IN

COST: $4 per hour or $20 per day

PRO TIP: If you get caught in a rip current, don't try to swim toward the shore. Instead, swim parallel to the shore until you're out of the current.

Michigan. A popular surfing spot on the Great Lake is at Whihala Beach by the BP Whiting Refinery, the largest inland oil refinery in the United States, though people also surf in East Chicago, Gary, Portage, and Michigan City. When conditions are optimal, they paddle into the icy lake, ride the whitecaps, and sometimes return with icicles hanging from their beards. You have to be pretty hardcore to surf in the Region. "It only calls the people who really want to do it," East Side native and longtime surfer Peter Matushek told *The South Side Weekly*. "I think the lighthearted surfers—it's just not for them."

THE BAILLY HOMESTEAD AT INDIANA DUNES NATIONAL PARK

How can you see how the Region's early settlers lived?

You can learn about the trappers, traders, and farmers who first settled Northwest Indiana in the 1800s at the Indiana Dunes National Park's Bailly Homestead, the last extant remnant of the fur trade that brought European settlers to the Region. The National Historic Landmark near Porter preserves the way of life of some of Northwest Indiana's pioneers. You can visit the home of Joseph Bailly, a trader who played a significant part in the development of the Calumet Region. One of Northwest Indiana's earliest known settlers, he set up a fur trading post in 1822 near the Little Calumet River at the crossroads of the Sauk Trail and other paths used by Native Americans. His 2,000-acre homestead, the last of its kind left in Northwest Indiana, served as a rest stop for travelers between Chicago and Detroit during the 19th century.

Subsequent owners supplied timber when the railroads came, bringing in Swedish immigrants from Chicago to chop down trees and run the sawmill. Visitors can see 19th-century

Left: *A Park Ranger guides a tour of the Bailly Homestead at the Indiana Dunes National Park.*

Right: *The fur trader Joseph Bailly was one of the earliest European settlers of Northwest Indiana.*

log cabins and the Bailly House that was hewn from oak and cedar in the rustic vernacular architecture of the time. You pass by a working farm with cows, chickens, and pigs wallowing in the mud at the neighboring Chellberg Farm before hiking a short distance to the homestead. You can take a guided tour every Sunday afternoon during the summer and get a look inside the homestead's historic buildings. It includes a trek out to the Bailly Cemetery, a family graveyard less than a mile away on the edge of a sand ridge at the highest point in the area on a bluff that once overlooked Lake Michigan. Several members of the Bailly family and Swedish residents from the area are buried under the shadow of a tall cross on the elevated cemetery platform.

The annual Midsommar Festival held at the Bailly Homestead celebrates the cultural heritage of the Swedish immigrants who settled in the area. Yes, there's the raising of and dancing around a maypole. No, it's nothing like the horror film.

IDEAL SECTION
OF HIGHWAY

Where can you find an ideal section of highway?

In the 19th century, roads in America were largely rugged, erratic, and unreliable during a "Dark Ages of road building." An "Ideal Section" of the Lincoln Highway set out to change that. Indianapolis Motor Speedway investor and headlight maker Carl G. Fisher conceived of the transcontinental highway named in honor of Abraham Lincoln as a way to sell more cars and connect the country, making it possible to drive from New York City to San Francisco. Designed by famed landscape architect Jens Jensen at the commission of Edsel Ford, the Ideal Section was built in Dyer in 1923. It was smooth, well-lit, and wide, with room for pulling over and resting. The Lincoln Highway Association, United Rubber Company, and Portland Cement Association consulted with 17 of the country's top highway experts to conceive of the "seedling mile"—actually 1.3 to 1.5 miles—meant to demonstrate the construction of good roads and be a model to be emulated all over the country. Hailed as a vision of the future, the ideal highway featured thick steel-reinforced cement and top-of-the-line infrastructure like curbs, culverts, sidewalks, and landscaping. Unlike most of the narrow, unimproved roads of its era, the prototype reached 40 feet wide with 100 feet of right-of-way.

The monument by Meyer's Castle has a lot more to see than the actual remaining stretch of the Ideal Section of Highway. Three historical panels, complete with photos and detailed timelines, are about as long as a novel, explaining the history in depth.

IDEAL SECTION OF HIGHWAY

WHAT: Historic sign and monument

WHERE: 1250 Joliet St., Dyer, IN; park on Northwinds Dr.

COST: Free

PRO TIP: Watch for traffic as it's just off a busy highway where cars whip by constantly.

Top: *Most roads were pretty rough when this was the ideal section of highway.*

Inset: *A monument honors the legacy of the Lincoln Highway's Ideal Section.*

It's now indistinguishable from any other highway to give you some idea of how rough road conditions were for motorists back then. Only about 2.5 percent of the 2.2 million miles of rural roads in America were paved at the time. The Ideal Section was intended to have a campsite at a time when most long-distance travelers paid farmers to park and sleep in their fields, but it ended up scuttled because of the cost. All that remains today is some signage along US 30 and a historical marker, but the Ideal Section nonetheless remains "a large part of Northwest Indiana's history."

BARKER MANSION BLACKOUT TOUR

How can you go on a Victorian ghost tour?

Traditionally, around Halloween every year since 2016, the Barker Mansion in Michigan City hosts a blackout tour that has nothing to do with imbibing too much liquor. It's not a ghost tour or haunted house like many that spring up during that time of year, just a dimming of the lights in the historic mansion. It is, after all, how people lived when the mansion was built in the 19th century. The dark adds a lot of spooky ambiance as befitting the Halloween season at the English Manor–style house that was built by railroad tycoon John H. Barker in 1857 and is now listed on the National Register of Historic Places. The museum gets immersed in near-total darkness, with only faint sources of illumination coming from tea lights and glow stick necklaces. Interpretive guides recount "unusual and eerie historic happenings," such as ghost trains, the haunted lighthouse, the ghost of Diana of the Dunes, and other local folklore that's held a fascination for many.

"The purpose of the Blackout Tours is not to scare or frighten anyone," Barker Mansion Interim Director Jessica Rosier told *The Times of Northwest Indiana*. "There will not be zombies or ghosts popping out, and there will be no paranormal equipment. These tours are,

---

BARKER MANSION

WHAT: Home to annual Blackout Tours

WHERE: 631 Washington St., Michigan City, IN

COST: $15 for adults and $10 for kids

PRO TIP: Make an evening of it by grabbing a bite at one of Michigan City's fine restaurants like Fish Camp, the Polish Peasant, Fiddlehead, Leeds Public House, or the Hokkaido Sushi Restaurant.

Top: *The Barker Mansion hosts Blackout Tours every October.*

Inset: *The Barker Mansion offers less spooky tours year-round.*

however, a chance to view history from a much different angle." Barker Mansion Assistant Director TJ Kalin came up with the idea when he realized how many visitors would appreciate seeing first-hand what happens there when the lights are off since so many inquire about ghosts at the Gilded Age–era house. "A lot of people ask if the mansion is haunted," Kalin told *The Times*. "We don't talk about that on normal tours, since our primary purpose is to interpret the Barker legacy. People are still curious, though, so that's why we created the Blackout Tours."

The Blackout Tours are intended to be a way to interpret folklore and discuss the origins of the haunted Victorian mansion stereotype without scaring guests. Tickets are available by calling 219-873-1520 or visiting barkermansion.com.

THOMAS EDISON'S OLD OFFICE

Where did Thomas Edison once work while helping design one of America's greatest engineering landmarks?

Thomas Edison once worked out of the Archway Building of the former State Line Generating Plant at the border of Hammond and Chicago. The coal-fired plant, built in 1929 during a time of national urbanization and an electricity boom, has been described as an engineering and architectural marvel but also was one of the worst polluters in Chicagoland before it was decommissioned. It's since been replaced with a much cleaner data center, but the Art Deco Archway Building that was the entrance to the plant and was where Edison once took part in plant design meetings remains. Designed by the same architecture firm that designed the Fields Museum, the Shedd Aquarium, the Wrigley Building, and the Chicago Civic Opera House, the building can be viewed while on a hike or visiting the nearby Hammond Bird Sanctuary or Hammond Beach.

The generators at the now-defunct State Line Generating Plant were personally designed by Edison. He worked with his protégé Samuel Insull, the CEO of the Commonwealth Edison company that's now known as ComEd, to build the world's largest turbine generator, which could produce 208,000 kilowatts of energy or 30 percent more than the second-most productive generator in the world. The plant's Unit 1 generator was the best in the world for 25 years, providing energy to more than a million homes across Chicagoland. It helped electrify homes and businesses from the city to the rural farmlands beyond the outskirts of the suburbs. The plant was one of the oldest continuously operating urban power plants in the world but was eventually closed by Dominion Resources in 2012.

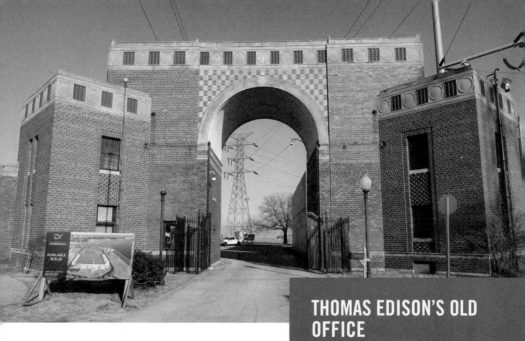

Thomas Edison attended design meetings at the Archway Building while helping design the now-razed State Line Generating Plant.

THOMAS EDISON'S OLD OFFICE

WHAT: Art Deco entrance to historic power plant

WHERE: Archway Building at Digital Crossroads Data Center at 1 Digital Crossroads, Hammond, IN

COST: Free

PRO TIP: Trek a little further west to Calumet Park in Chicago which has a nice cultural center, and stroll along the lakefront.

Reduced to just 100 employees after repeated Clear Air Act violations, it was deemed too costly to keep running up to modern environmental standards. It had been a major source of greenhouse gases, nitrogen oxide, sulfur dioxide, and toxic mercury.

The American Society of Mechanical Engineers ranked the State Line Generating Plant as the 24th-most significant landmark in engineering history, leading the gateway to become an international icon in advertising for advancements in power generation.

CANDY CANE LANE

Where can you travel down Candy Cane Lane?

The Region, which inspired Jean Shepherd's *A Christmas Story*, is filled with Christmas magic like Peteyville in Hammond, the Magical Light Show in Dyer, and Christmas on 124th Ave. in Winfield. In Crown Point, there's a whole block of homes decorated for Christmas, complete with massive pine trees, oversized inflatables, a huge leg lamp, and 6-foot-tall wooden candy canes. Every house on the Candy Cane Lane block contributes to the annual Christmas display that's been described as a "fairyland." It's a magical experience many Region residents drive through and stop to photograph.

The holiday tradition started in 1958 on Holton Ridge when homeowners first decided to adorn the cul-de-sac with white bamboo candy canes they stripped with red reflective tape and set out two feet apart. The candy canes glowed in the headlights of passing cars. Carolers flocked there in the early days because elaborate Christmas decorations weren't as common at the time. Serving doughnuts and drinks to participants, the neighbors gathered in their garages every year to plan that year's display until the group became a well-oiled machine. The decorations grew and grew over the years to include Christmas trees, a Nativity scene with a star, Santa in a sleigh, and many reindeer, including a giant Rudolph. Each lawn holds new wonders that turn heads as a steady procession of cars cruise slowly by every December. The twinkling lights evoke a

CANDY CANE LANE

WHAT: Entire block of Christmas decorations

WHERE: Holton Ridge in Crown Point, IN

COST: Free

PRO TIP: If weather permits, park and get out of your car and stroll around the street to better take in the magical atmosphere and get a good look at the decorations.

Candy Cane Lane is an entire cul-de-sac of homes that decorate every Christmas season.

sense of holiday magic that will put anyone in the Christmas spirit. People flock from all over to visit, many making the pilgrimage at least once every year. As longtime resident Scott Fulk told *The Times of Northwest Indiana*, "If somebody asks where we live in Crown Point, if we say 'Holton Ridge,' no one knows where we mean. If we say 'Candy Cane Lane,' they immediately know. It is a Crown Point institution."

Candy Cane Lane has been delighting people with its holiday magic for more than 60 years. There's no written covenant that binds new homeowners to participate in the decorating, just an understanding that—when they move onto the block—they will join in the fun.

125

NEW YEAR'S EVE PIEROGI DROP

Where does a Pierogi drop 60 feet on New Year's Eve?

The United States is filled with weird New Year's Eve celebrations, including a peach drop in Atlanta, a conch drop in Key West, and a disco ball drop in Baltimore. In the Region, Whiting drops a massive pierogi to ring in the New Year. The industrial lakefront city is known for the annual summer Pierogi Fest celebration that draws more than 350,000 people downtown over the course of a weekend to celebrate the humble Eastern European dumpling. The revelry continues on New Year's Eve with the annual drop of an illuminated 10-foot-tall pierogi into a boiling cooking pot at the stroke of midnight. Yes, the Pierogi Drop is completely ridiculous and it's meant to be. "When you tell people you're dropping a lit-up 10-foot pierogi 90 feet, they immediately get a smile on their face," event chairman Andy Dybel told *The Times of Northwest Indiana*, saying the hope was "to steal a little bit of the Pierogi Fest thunder."

The Whiting Knights of Columbus Pierogi Drop takes place at the corner of Atchison and 119th Streets. Kicking off at 8 p.m. on New Year's Eve, it's free with hours of live music leading up to the big countdown, which is followed by an after-party where the beer flows freely at the Knights of Columbus Hall. The

---

The Knights of Columbus Hall, also a popular watering hole during Pierogi Fest, operates a beer garden on New Year's Eve where you can grab Polish sausage, Italian beef, and of course, pierogi. Father Time has even made appearances with Baby New Year.

Why drop a ball on New Year's Eve when you can drop a pierogi?

PIEROGI DROP

WHAT: New Year's Eve party, Polish-style

WHERE: 1120 119th St., Whiting, IN

COST: Free

PRO TIP: Whiting is closely associated with the filled dumpling because of Pierogi Fest and is also known for the many taverns. New Year's Eve revelers can wet their whistle at Brewdog Brewery, the Standard Taproom, the Clipper, the Office, Portside Pub, and the venerable Center Lounge.

festivities include food trucks, a giant countdown clock, a rousing rendition of "Auld Lang Syne," and a fireworks show staged by Krazy Kaplans. Thousands of revelers typically throng the street, which is closed to traffic. If you don't feel like braving the cold or staying out that late, the local radio station WJOB typically livestreams the Whiting Knights of Columbus Council 1696's annual party. If you're crazy enough, there's often a No Fee, No Tee Polar Plunge at Whihala Beach the next day.

FIGHTER JET OFF THE OAK SAVANNAH TRAIL

Why does an old fighter jet stand sentry in someone's backyard?

A 2.4-mile stretch of the Oak Savannah Trail in Hobart is part of the Indiana Dunes National Park and the Hobart Nature District, which also includes Robinson Lake and the Hobart Woods Trail. The trail takes people past horse farms, oak trees, and forests filled with white-tail deer and other wildlife. An unexpected sight is the vintage T-33 jet used by the US Marine Corps for training missions during World War II. The plane journeyed from Chicago's Great Lakes Naval Station where sailors undergo basic training to the Hobart VFW branch to the home of Dick Boyd, a Marine Corps veteran who served as vice president of the century-old Boyd Construction and whose father built the Lake George Dam. Boyd, who was not a pilot but served in the Marine Corps Reserves for nine years, bought the T-33 plane for a dollar and some construction materials in 1975.

The jet now rests behind a copse of trees in the backyard of Boyd's four-story house, where it has served as a point of local interest and a clubhouse for his kids. It sits just off the popular trail where it can be seen and

FIGHTER JET IN A BACKYARD

WHAT: Decommissioned World War II plane where you'd least suspect it

WHERE: 5253 S Liverpool Rd., Hobart, IN, just off the Oak Savannah Trail. There's a nearby trailhead at Robinson Lake Park

COST: Free

PRO TIP: There are several military vehicles to see around the Region, such as the tanks along main roads in Griffith and Crown Point and the Vietnam-era Huey medevac helicopter at the Lansing Veterans Memorial.

A fighter jet seems a little out-of-place in a random backyard in Hobart.

photographed by passersby. Keep walking along the trail; there will eventually be a break in the tree line that will afford a good vantage point for viewing and taking pictures. It's an unusual landmark to stumble upon in a less developed part of town that's mostly farms and parkland. Boyd is not bothered when people stop to take pictures. He told *The Times of Northwest Indiana*: "It's everybody's, it's just registered to me." Having your own jet does have its perks though: "There's nothing better than on a hot summer night, grabbing a cold beer and laying on a cold aluminum wing and watching the stars," he told *The Times.*

The T-33 won't ever fly anywhere again. Its working points have been removed. But it's been trotted out for several parades, including a World War II commemoration where Boyd's daughter dressed as Rosie the Riveter while riding with the jet.

GRAVE OF OSCAR MAYER'S LITTLE OSCAR

Where can you visit the grave of the Wienermobile's last Little Oscar?

When the Oscar Mayer Wienermobile was first rolled out in the 1930s, the inside was so small it could only accommodate passengers of diminutive stature. Northwest Indiana native George Molchan, who "stood only 10 hot dogs high" despite taking hormone supplements as a kid in a bid to grow taller, got hired to crisscross the country in the iconic hot dog–shaped car. He served as the longest-reigning Oscar Mayer spokesperson "Little Oscar" and became a "towering figure in the annals of mid-20th century adversity." For decades he traveled around the country in a chef's toque passing out hot dog–shaped Magic Wiener Whistles to kids at supermarkets, festivals, and parades, later greeting visitors at Oscar Mayer's restaurant at Disney World in Florida. He landed the gig after meeting the original Little Oscar, Meinhardt Raabe, who also played the Munchkin in *The Wizard of Oz* who announced the death of the Wicked Witch of the East.

Molchan accumulated many stories while on the road, including one about some college students who slathered the Wienermobile in mustard and one featuring a state trooper who pulled them over because he wanted to take a picture. His

Though the Little Oscar Mascot has been retired, the Oscar Mayer Wienermobile rolls on. The iconic, hot dog–shaped car still makes frequent visits to local Strack & Van Til supermarkets for special occasions.

Little Oscar George Molchan is buried in Merrillville.

GEORGE "LITTLE OSCAR" MOLCHAN'S GRAVESTONE

WHAT: Final resting place of Oscar Mayer spokesmanç

WHERE: Calumet Park Cemetery at 2305 W 73rd Ave., Merrillville, IN

COST: Free

PRO TIP: Ask for directions as the ground-level grave is hard to find. For more information, call 219-769-8803.

Weinermobile, based in Chicago, was even stolen once on a trip to Cleveland, though it was quickly recovered. He most enjoyed visiting kids in children's hospitals and seeing their eyes light up. When Molchan retired in 1987, the company also retired the Little Oscar character that he embodied so completely. He died in 2005 and mourners sang "Oh, I wish I were an Oscar Mayer wiener" at his funeral. Molchan's gravestone can be viewed in the Calumet Park Cemetery in Merrillville just north of the intersection of US 30 and Taft Street. The gates are open from dawn to dusk and anyone can track down the headstone in Section 19, at Marker 901.

FLORIDA TROPICAL HOUSE

Why is a Florida-style house on a ridgeline overlooking Lake Michigan?

Though the Hoosier State is often thought of as landlocked, Northwest Indiana has a spectacular coastline. That's nowhere more clear than in Beverly Shores, where the Century of Progress Homes were ferried across Lake Michigan from the 1933 World's Fair in Chicago. Developer Robert Bartlett shipped them by barge across Lake Michigan to Beverly Shores, a coastal resort town he was building on the Indiana shoreline that's now more of a suburban bedroom community. The experimental homes are so modern that they still look futuristic (save for the rustic Cypress Log house).

They line a stretch of Lake Shore Drive overlooking Lake Michigan. The Cypress Log, Wieboldt-Rostone, and Armco-Ferro houses all showcase new-fangled building materials that never ultimately caught on. Most stunning of all is the flamingo-colored Florida Tropical House that was actually commissioned by the state of Florida to promote the allure of its laid-back beach living. The bright pastel home stands on a sweeping bluff overlooking Kemil Beach and the boundless horizon of Lake Michigan. It's a striking image that looks completely out-of-place in Indiana and more like it belongs on a postcard. Like the other Century of Progress homes, it's

FLORIDA TROPICAL HOUSE

WHAT: Century of Progress Home

WHERE: 210 Lake Front Dr., Beverly Shores, IN

COST: Free

PRO TIP: Make sure to get tickets for the Century of Progress homes tours as soon as they go on sale as they sell out quickly.

The Florida House overlooks Lake Michigan in Beverly Shores.

privately owned so as to ensure its ongoing care and maintenance. But it's still a popular destination, especially for those headed to nearby Indiana Dunes National Park sites like Boater's Beach or the Great Marsh Trail. You can park in 15-minute spots, take photos, and read the highly detailed interpretative signs that explain each house. It's worth walking all the way behind the Florida Tropical House as it looks beautiful against the bright blue Lake Michigan backdrop.

Indiana Landmarks leads a tour through the Century of Progress homes once a year in October so you can see the inside while contributing to the homes' preservation. Park rangers and volunteers lead visitors through the first floor of each, explaining the architecture and history.

JACKSON FAMILY TRIBUTE AT HARD ROCK CASINO

How did the Jackson 5 museum that was never built come about in a roundabout way?

A 37-foot-tall and 15-foot-wide guitar marquee looms outside the Hard Rock Casino just off the Borman Expressway in Gary. It's modeled after the 1965 Airline Town and Country guitar owned by former steelworker Joe Jackson, whose children used to form The Jackson 5. The King of Pop hailed from humble origins in the Steel City, where his childhood home has been preserved as a landmark that still draws visitors, especially on his birthday and the anniversary of his death. Other landmarks of his time haven't been so lucky. The Gary Memorial Auditorium where the Jackson 5 performed and won a talent show was largely destroyed in the Great Gary Arson of 1997 save for a grand entrance that met the wrecking ball last year. Mister Lucky's Lounge, a nightclub where they played in the early days, has long been abandoned and fallen into disrepair. A four-story mural of the Jackson 5 downtown got razed.

The family talked for a long time about building a Michael Jackson Museum along with a performing arts center, golf course, and other attractions, but it never happened. However,

---

The Jackson 5 first performed at Mister Lucky's Lounge, a combination liquor store and bar at 1100 Grant Street in Gary. They sang covers of The Temptations and James Brown there before the family decamped for Detroit to start their career.

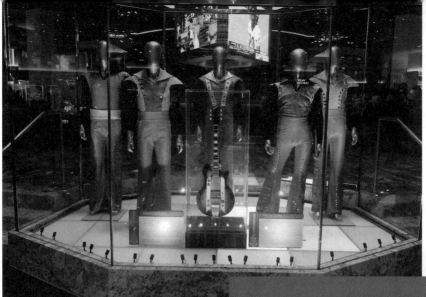

The new Hard Rock Casino in Gary displays a lot of Jackson 5 memorabilia.

a semblance of the much-touted Jackson Museum finally came to fruition just south of the Borman Expressway, just two exits away from where the museum was supposed to go. The new Hard Rock Casino is packed with music memorabilia, including John Mellencamp's hand-written lyrics to "Small Town," the Arby's hat Pharrell wore while performing "Happy" at the Grammys, and the Spider-Man socks Wilco frontman Jeff Tweedy wore. It also pays tribute to Gary musicians including Queen of House Music Kym Mazelle. There's an extensive section devoted to the Jackson family, including several of their stage outfits. There's memorabilia in the Hard Rock Cafe and scattered throughout the casino floor, as well as an entire Jackson 5 exhibit in the performing arts venue that hosts concerts.

EDISON CONCEPT HOUSES

Can a tribute to a famous rapper save Thomas Edison's worker housing?

Thomas Alva Edison was an incredibly prolific inventor. Though best known for coming up with the light bulb, motion picture projector, and phonograph, he filed an average of one patent every 14 days for four decades. One of his eureka moments paved the way for building all-concrete houses. US Steel, which had founded a fast-growing company town around its Gary Works steel mill, saw Edison's concept homes as a solution to that housing shortage that forced its workers to shack up in shanties, boarding houses, and other less-than-satisfactory accommodations. A US Steel subsidiary used Edison's formed concrete molds to construct row houses for workers and standalone cottages for managers. A total of 86 Edison Concept Houses were constructed between 1910 and 1913 on the north side of the Steel City, where workers could walk to their jobs at the mill.

The project eventually petered out after the construction method was deemed too costly. Only about 72 of the houses remain today. Some are occupied but many are abandoned and have become dilapidated. Indiana University Northwest Director of Arts Programming and Engagement, Lauren Pacheco, has been seeking to call attention to preservation efforts through

---

FREDDIE GIBBS MURAL ON EDISON CONCEPT HOUSES

WHAT: A tribute to acclaimed rapper on historic worker housing

WHERE: 424 Monroe St., Gary, IN

COST: Free

PRO TIP: Visit destinationgary.com to see more of the #paintgary mural sites

The graffiti artist OverUnder painted murals on the Edison Concept Houses in Gary that attracted acclaim from the art world.

her #PaintGary project. She commissioned two murals at either end of a block of row houses on Monroe Street that included a portrait of the Grammy-nominated rapper Freddie Gibbs, a Gary native. Argentinian street artist Nicolas "Ever" Escalada painted the *United Steel Life* mural featuring a steel mill cafeteria and the El Frio pop once made in Gary. Erik Burke (a.k.a. OverUnder) painted wraparound murals of Gibbs in profile and a silhouetted head emerging from a rippling red sea on the other end that the Brooklyn Street Art website hailed as "stunning." The murals have become local landmarks, calling attention to Pacheco's aspirations to save the historic homes.

The Edison Concept Houses were built in four clusters in Gary: the Polk Street Cottages, Jackson Terraces, Monroe Terrace, and Van Buren Terrace. They were built floor-by-floor instead of with the single pour Edison envisioned.

NUDIST CLUBS

Where do free-range nudes run wild in Northwest Indiana?

People bare all at the Ponderosa Sun Club and the Sun Aura Club in Roselawn, and at the Lake O' The Woods Nudist Colony in Valparaiso. Dating as far back as the 1930s, the long-running nudist colonies give people the chance to be in the buff out in public. The Sun Aura Club has a famous landmark 25-foot-tall sundial in the shape of a woman's leg near the entrance. Founded as the Zoro Nudist Colony in 1933 by the Austrian attorney Alois Knapp and his wife Lorena, who also launched the National Nudist Council and published the nudist magazine *Sunshine and Health*, the colony has cycled through many names throughout the years, including "Club Bare," "Adam and Eve Community," "Naked City," and "Sun Spot."

The nearby Ponderosa Sun Club has hosted celebrities like Tim Allen, Vanilla Ice, Blues Traveler singer John Popper, Verne Troyer, Mancow Muller, and John Wayne Bobbitt, who often turn up at its annual Nudes-A-Poppin' pageant. Lake O' The Woods claims to be the second-longest operating naturist club in the United States and has the motto: "Shed your clothes and shed your worries." Generations of curious teenagers once parked near the gates in the hope of getting a glimpse, likely not realizing those who belong to such clubs tend to skew older. The Ponderosa Sun Club, which is filled with summer cottages, has public weekends twice a year to try to interest thousands of guests in losing their inhibitions and their clothes. Founded

---

You do not have to be a member to visit the clubs. If just curious, both of the Roselawn clubs offer daily passes. They do, however, ban cameras, video equipment, and usually clothes.

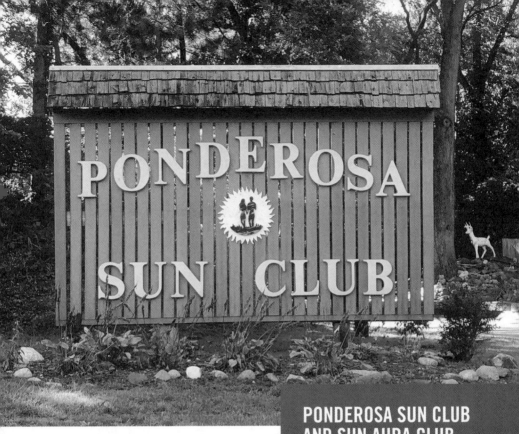

The Ponderosa Sun Club is not for the inhibited.

in 1964 a few miles from the Interstate 65 exit, it's been trying to draw in younger members for a lifestyle that's more commonly accepted in Europe. The resort-like clubs feature pools, lakes, hedges, flowers, statues, and recreational facilities like those found in campgrounds. They've even hosted nude weddings.

PONDEROSA SUN CLUB AND SUN AURA CLUB

WHAT: Nudist clubs

WHERE: 10600 N 400 E, Roselawn, IN; 3499 IN-10, Roselawn, IN

COST: Daily admission ranges from $20 to $25

PRO TIP: A Ponderosa Sun Club Q&A encourages visitors to bring "sunscreen, lounge chair, towel, tennis racquet, balls. Remember, clothing is not optional."

FORMER POW CAMP AT SWEET WOODS

Where can you visit a POW camp where Nazis once picked onions?

Northwest Indiana straddles the south suburban Chicago suburbs like Glenwood, renowned for the long-running Glenwood Oaks Rib and Chop House that *Chicago* magazine declared had Chicagoland's best ribs. The community also is home to the Sweet Woods, a Cook County Forest Preserve that was once home to the Civilian Conservation Corps camp that housed the down-and-out during the Great Depression, Illiana Christian High School for a year, and German prisoners captured during World War II who were dispatched to pick onions in Lansing, work at a fertilizer plant in Calumet City, and pickle onions in neighboring South Holland.

The POW camp has been largely demolished but a historical marker by the entrance of the forest preserve at 183rd Street and Cottage Grove Avenue explains what happened there. Camp Thornton was erected in 1934 to host the CCC, which President Franklin Roosevelt launched to employ the jobless during the New Deal. CCC workers who lived in the barracks there, mostly hailing from hard-hit rural communities in southern Illinois, planted trees, paved roads, and built shelters

It might be hard to envision Nazi prisoners toiling in south suburban farm fields but as Illinois State Historical Society Board Member Eliane Egdorf told *The Times of Northwest Indiana*: "People think that history happens somewhere else. History did happen right here."

A German POW camp was located in the Sweet Woods Forest Preserve in Glenwood.

SWEET WOODS

WHAT: Site of World War II POW camp

WHERE: 183rd St. and Cottage Grove Ave., Glenwood, IL

COST: Free

PRO TIP: Follow the trail along Thorn Creek, where the bluffs provide some dramatic views.

in the forest preserve, earning $31 a month. The camp was used to house German prisoners of war in 1945 and 1946, housing prisoners who were brought in from Africa. As many as 400 German soldiers were imprisoned there, which few neighbors were aware of at the time. The last remnants of Camp Thornton were razed in 1989, but you can still see the foundations by the historical marker. It's a great site for hiking, especially along the bluffs with sweeping views of Thorn Creek. The woods are filled with rope swings, rustic log bridges, and rough-hewn fences carved from trees. Try to make it all the way to the steel-truss pedestrian bridge that makes for excellent Instagram photos. If you're lucky, you might even see raptors soaring overhead.

GRANT STREET MARSH

What's a prime birding spot surrounded by truck stops?

A company town suffering from decades of depopulation and disinvestment, Gary's a strange place. Drive south on the Grant Street exit off the Borman Expressway and turn right on a soft gravel road off 32nd Avenue at the second stoplight. There's limited, unmarked parking by the water's edge. As you pull up to the Grant Street Marsh, it's like a Disney princess movie with birds flitting everywhere. Birds soar overhead, skit across the marsh, and alight on the countless reeds along the shoreline. Not far from the Indiana Dunes, it's an ideal spot to see waterfowl, red-winged blackbirds, and Great Blue Herons. One birder has described it as the crème de la crème of birding. Early in the spring, migrating pelicans have been known to stop there as well.

Birders have spotted more than 200 species at the marsh, including the Black-billed Cuckoo, American Avocet, White-rumped Sandpiper, Least Bittern, and the Bald Eagle. The

GRANT STREET MARSH

WHAT: Birders' paradise nestled between truck stops

WHERE: 32nd Ave. and Grant St., Gary, IN

COST: Free

PRO TIP: Watch out for all the bird poop on the trail and the occasional ATV rider roaring by.

The Region has many birding hotspots like the Seidner Dune & Swale Nature Preserve, Jeorse Park Beach, Johnson Beach, Miller Beach, Mount Baldy, Wolf Lake, George Lake, Roxana Pond, Gleason Park, the Gibson Woods, and the Hammond Cinder Flats.

The Grant Street Marsh is a prime birding spot hidden in an unlikely location.

ambiance is peaceful and the chirping constant. The marsh is surrounded by a 7,000-foot levee with a paved path that allows unobstructed observation from about 10 feet above water level along the south and east sides. The further west you go the more the marsh is filled with reeds for birds to flit about on. It's a quiet, contemplative trail to which you should bring an Audubon guidebook, binoculars, and a camera with a long lens. It's recommended that birders bring a spotting scope to best cover the entire area. You can see quite a distance as there are few trees in the levee to obstruct the view. The Grand Street Marsh is a designated Indiana Birding Trail site and one of the stops during the Indiana Dunes Birding Festival. The Dunes-Calumet Audubon Society and the Shirley Heinze Land Trust periodically lead guided tours there.

MICHAEL JORDAN MURAL

Where can you witness Michael Jordan sinking the NBA Finals–winning shot over Byron Russell for all eternity?

Legendary Region graffiti artist Felix "Flex" Maldonado has created some classic Northwest Indiana murals, including the four-story Jackson 5 mural in downtown Gary. At the commission of longtime Bulls fan Oscar Juarez, he immortalized a classic Chicago sports moment on the outside walls of OJ's Game Over Bar in East Chicago. Maldonado recreated the final moment of the most-watched game in National Basketball Association history, the culmination of Michael Jordan's illustrious career, and the end of one of the most dominant championship runs in history. Jordan stole the ball from behind Karl Malone in Game 6 at the Delta Center in Salt Lake City, dribbled down the court, and beat Jazz defender Byron Russell with a wicked crossover and step-back. He swished a 20-foot jump shot with little more than five seconds left on the clock, notching 45 points and his 25th game-winner while in a Chicago Bulls uniform. The six-peat capped his unbeatable legacy.

Maldonado splashed the scene over the entire building, depicting the Jazz fans frozen in disbelief in a largely abstract and out-of-focus black-and-white way to avoid copyright

---

Michael Jordan, then a much-hyped draft pick, played his first game in a Bulls uniform in Washington High School in East Chicago. He squared off in the preseason exhibition against the Milwaukee Bucks. The gymnasium has since been razed.

Michael Jordan's sixth championship-clinching final shot as a Bull is forever immortalized in a mural on the side of an East Chicago bar.

MICHAEL JORDAN MURAL

WHAT: Muralist's tribute to "The Last Shot"

WHERE: OJ's Game Over Bar at 710 W 151st St., East Chicago, IN

COST: Free

PRO TIP: Seek out other Felix "Flex" Maldonado murals around the Region, including at Wolf Lake, the Hammond Environmental Center, and Emilio's Restaurante & Cantina.

infringements from the original photo. Maldonado and assistant Lisa Jones spent about six weeks painting the mural, braving 40-degree winter weather. He decided to re-appropriate a second-floor apartment mural to serve as a backboard. The mural pops. Jordan and the ball are depicted in color while the whole background is in black-and-white to heighten the dramatic effect. People have frequently stopped there, often pulling over on the spot, to take pictures of the instant landmark. Located along the heavily trafficked Indianapolis Boulevard and described by the artist as a "mini tourist attraction," it's also been a popular spot for selfies and music videos. The work has scored a lot of acclaim, including from Artist Replete, which described it as "one of the greatest Michael Jordan murals we've ever seen."

BEVERLY SHORES DEPOT MUSEUM AND ART GALLERY

Why is an old train station partly an art gallery?

Located in a historic pink stucco train station, the Beverly Shores Depot Museum and Art Gallery hosts exhibits both educational and artistic. You can learn about beachfront erosion along Lake Michigan or see paintings by a local artist. Then you could catch a train to Chicago or South Bend as it's actually still a working train station and a must-stop destination along the Dunes Highway when it's open on weekends from May to October. The Depot is located in the Broadway South Shore Line Station that was built in 1929. The building was placed on the National Register of Historic Places in 1989 and renovated during the 1990s as a result of the preservation efforts that followed the closing of the beachfront town's other South Shore Line station.

Opened in 1998, the Depot Museum typically features the work of local artists, including paintings, sculpture, photography, hand-blown glasswork, and mixed media between May and October. It also has exhibitions highlighting the history of the town that was developed as a lakefront resort community by Fred and Robert Bartlett. Named

BEVERLY SHORES DEPOT MUSEUM AND ART GALLERY

WHAT: Museum in a working train station

WHERE: 525 S Broadway, Beverly Shores, IN

COST: Free

PRO TIP: You're just a few steps from the Beverly Shores History Trail that teaches you about the town's past and the Calumet Trail where you might see Great Blue Herons, wild turkeys, and stalks of *Lobelia inflata* (also called Indian Tobacco).

Top: *The Beverly Shores Depot Museum and Art Gallery is located in a working train station.*

Inset: *The museum chronicles the history of the resort town.*

for Robert's daughter, the town was laid out just before the Great Depression but was never built out as much as was envisioned, so most of the land eventually ended up becoming part of the Indiana Dunes National Park. Historic exhibits have focused on homes displayed by the park, Lithuanian immigration, and Beverly Shores's war veterans. Situated on the main road into town, the museum and art gallery is a community gathering place where you can nosh on cheese while mingling at the art opening receptions. It's especially hopping on Second Fridays and its annual 5x5 fundraiser in which people pay $55 to buy a donated artwork measuring 5" x 5". The gift shop also carries many unique items from local artisans.

Pop across the street to the Rolling Stonebaker Pizza Truck or the Goblin and the Grocer, an upscale restaurant with a wine bar, coffee shop, and small selection of well-curated groceries from local suppliers like The Wurst butcher shop.

OGDEN DUNES SKI JUMP

How did one of the largest ski jumps in the Midwest end up in flat Indiana?

Indiana is known for being a topographically challenged state. Renowned for its flatness, it's not exactly a hotspot for ski bunnies looking to hit the slopes. But the beachfront town of Ogden Dunes in Porter County—which was founded by millionaire sand-miner Francis A. Ogden but which ended up birthing the Save the Dunes preservationist movement—was however once home to a ski jump that was billed as the highest in the United States. The Grand Beach Ski Club operated on one of the highest dunes in town in the 1920s and 1930s. The monstrous jump was built along the crest of the hill with the intent of shattering world records. The engineer estimated skiers would jump at more than 60 miles per hour, then the top speed of the best-selling Ford Model A. The 192-foot-tall ski jump held meets and hosted the medal-winning Norwegian Olympic team. Skiers rocketed down a slope 30 stories tall before soaring 100 feet over spectators' heads. As many as 20,000 people attended sometimes.

It grew into enough of an attraction that it was immortalized in a South Shore Line poster. The longest jump ever recorded off the tower was 195 feet. Backers hoped the death-defying ski jumping would help bring more attractions to the small duneland town that then had streets made of sand. But the

---

Ogden Dunes seems like a restricted community as it often has a greeter outside its front gate. Though it has no businesses or public beach parking, the hilly bedroom community has more than a dozen architecturally distinguished homes worth seeing.

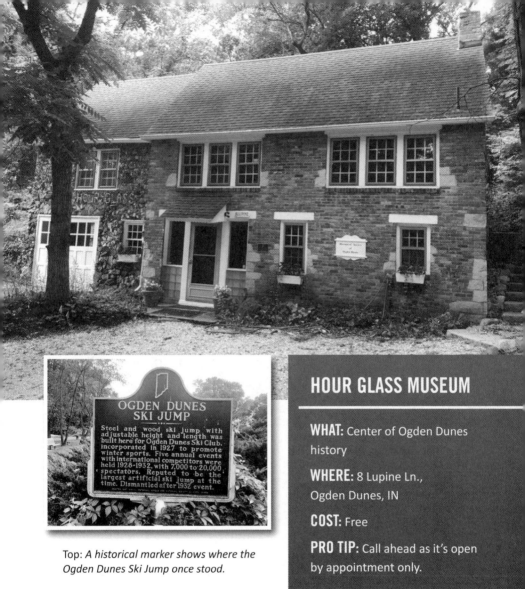

OGDEN DUNES
SKI JUMP

Steel and wood ski jump with adjustable height and length was built here for Ogden Dunes Ski Club. Incorporated in 1927 to promote winter sports. Five annual events with international competitors were held 1928-1932, with 7,000 to 20,000 spectators. Reputed to be the largest artificial ski jump at the time. Dismantled after 1932 event.

HOUR GLASS MUSEUM

WHAT: Center of Ogden Dunes history

WHERE: 8 Lupine Ln., Ogden Dunes, IN

COST: Free

PRO TIP: Call ahead as it's open by appointment only.

Top: *A historical marker shows where the Ogden Dunes Ski Jump once stood.*

Inset: *The Ogden Dunes Ski Jump was immortalized with a South Shore Line poster.*

Great Depression took a financial toll, as did a lack of consistent snow. The club dismantled the steel-framed tower and sold it to a ski club where Olympic teams trained in Rockford, Illinois, until it was moved to Wisconsin. A few arts and crafts houses were built atop the dune to take advantage of the lakefront views. All that remains is a historical marker commemorating the site at the east end of Kratz Field and photographs that can be viewed at the Hour Glass Museum.

NATHAN MANILOW SCULPTURE PARK

Why is that towering Paul Bunyan so sad?

The Governor's State University sculpture walk in University Park bills itself as a museum in the prairie and it's no tall tale. The outdoor attraction presents world-class contemporary sculpture amid a varied natural landscape that encompasses tall grass and woods. The 100-acre Nathan Manilow Sculpture Park, colloquially known as The Nate, is accessible from dawn until dusk year-round. Wander the grounds tucked between a college campus and farm fields to see sculptures like *Phoenix*, *Rudder*, and *The Wishing Tree*. The main trail wends around a picturesque lake through prairie and other habitats. Oft-Instagrammed standouts include Jene Highstein's *Flying Saucer* and the towering sad *Paul Bunyan* at the edge of the prairie. The four-story-tall lumberjack sculpture crafted by artist Tony Tasset stands

NATHAN MANILOW SCULPTURE PARK

WHAT: Epic sculpture collection at Governors State University

WHERE: 1 University Dr., University Park, IL

COST: Free

PRO TIP: Make sure to budget a few hours to have enough time to trek around the entire grounds.

Tony Tasset's larger-than-life sculpture of the woodsman Paul Bunyan became The Nate's face when it was installed in 2006. The monumental 30-foot Paul is likely to resonate with people because it shows the folk hero in a vulnerable moment of fatigue.

Paul Bunyan needs a break.

stoop-shouldered, his ax sagging from chopping down so many trees. You can feel the hunched woodsman's sheer exhaustion. You won't weary of the sculpture park's ever-growing collection, which recently added Chicago artist Terry Karpowicz's 21-foot-tall *Stargazing with Contrails*. Forged from steel I-beams and fabricated steel, the piece points skyward with the aim of being "a moving tribute to summer on the prairie."

The Nate, also home to Karpowicz's Art Ark, hosts annual events like Sculpture, Wine & Dine every September and a Winter Walk followed by hot soup in mid-December. It bears visiting throughout the year because your perception of the sculptures can change with the seasons, standing out in sharper contrast in the winter, for instance. The Nate also has a free audio tour on the Otocast app that provides more information about each artwork on the grounds, with many of the audio clips recorded by the artists themselves. You also can grab a foldout paper map at the main entrance of the campus. The sculpture park can be visited from dawn to dusk 365 days a year and is always free and open to the public.

THE RUINS OF LONG-ABANDONED STEEL MILLS

Where can you see the remnants of what were once the world's two largest steel mills?

Northwest Indiana is steel country. More than 100,000 workers—many immigrants from Eastern Europe—once toiled in the mills along the lakeshore. It was said that everyone in the Region knew someone who worked at a steel mill. The major mills endured, producing as much steel as they ever did, but with a fraction of the number of employees. US Steel, the world's first billion-dollar company that was referenced as a symbol of the establishment in *The Godfather*, founded Gary as a company town in 1906. Its flagship Gary Works remains one of Northwest Indiana's largest employers, but its first foothold in the Calumet Region was South Works at the mouth of the Calumet River on Chicago's East Side.

The mill on Lake Michigan was the country's largest during the 19th century, once employing 20,000 workers and providing much of the metal for the skyscrapers downtown. It declined along with the rest of the steel industry, shuttering in 1992. Just 700 workers remained at the end. Today, part of the mill property has been turned into Steelworkers Park, a secluded spot on the lakefront with trails and a statue honoring the steelworkers who labored there for more than a century. The

The Joliet Iron Works helped expand the railroads in the late 19th and early 20th century, forging 2,000 tons of iron a day and employing about 4,000 workers at its height. The Forest Preserve occasionally offers guided tours.

One can explore the ruins of the Joliet Iron Works.

STEELWORKERS PARK AND JOLIET STEEL AND IRON WORKS

WHAT: Steel mill ruins

WHERE: E 87th St., Chicago or Columbia St., Joliet, IL

COST: Free

PRO TIP: When visiting Steelworkers Park, stop by the nearby Calumet Fisheries, the legendary smoked fish joint that's been spotlighted by Anthony Bourdain, has received a lifetime James Beard Award, and was recognized by CNN as one of the Top 10 Historic Restaurants in Chicago.

towering iron ore walls have been described as "American ruins." One section was converted into a climbing wall. Visitors can also see the industrial ruins of what was the second-largest steel mill in Joliet. The long-gone Joliet Iron Works was founded on the Des Plaines River in 1869, giving Joliet the nickname "City of Stone and Steel" and appearing in the classic sports movie *Rudy*. It's now a Forest Preserve District of Will County park. There's a self-guided tour along a trail with many interpretative signs. You can see the haunting stone remains of gas engine houses and blast furnaces that burned out long ago.

GOLDEN AGE CEDAR LAKE AT THE MUSEUM AT LASSEN'S RESORT

Where did gangsters once get away?

Chicago became the world's meatpacking capital before refrigeration. The Chicago Stockyards shipped meat by rail all over the country with ice harvested from local lakes in the winter. Armour & Company quarried the frozen surface of Cedar Lake in Northwest Indiana. It ran a boarding house on the lake where it brought in transient workers to cut ice for six to eight weeks. Hotelier Chris Lassen bought the building, moved it across the lake, and reopened it as the Lassen Resort Hotel in 1921. The 1920s were Cedar Lake's golden age as a summer playground. More than 50 resorts ringed the lake. People flocked there to fish, canoe, and ride steamboats after the Monon Railroad came to town. There were dance halls, saloons, and boxing matches. It was a popular getaway for Midwesterners including gangsters like Al Capone. The Lassen Hotel was a popular spot with a dance pavilion, toboggan slide, and restaurant on the lake. But the Great Depression put an end to the town's resort era.

MUSEUM AT LASSEN'S RESORT

WHAT: Homage to Cedar Lake's Golden Age

WHERE: 7408 Constitution Ave., Cedar Lake, IN

COST: $5 for people five years old and up

PRO TIP: After your visit, be sure to spend some time idling on a rocking chair on the porch enjoying the vast lakefront view while nostalgic 1920s music is piped in.

Left: *The Museum at Lassen's Resort traces the history of Cedar Lake back to the Ice Age.*

Right: *The arrival of the Monon Railroad transformed Cedar Lake into a resort town.*

The Lassen Hotel became a church camp while other resorts faded into oblivion. The town later bought the old hotel and the Cedar Lake Historical Association stepped in to save it and get it listed on the National Register of Historic Places when it was at risk of being razed. It opened The Lake of the Red Cedars Museum there to preserve the town's rich history, including how Dr. William Scholl got his start in shoemaking as his grandfather's apprentice in Cedar Lake. The museum recently underwent a $50,000 renovation project that left it looking like a million bucks. Rebranded as the Museum at Lassen's Resort, it now features the seven-room *Story of Cedar Lake* exhibit. You can find mastodon bones, vintage ice cutting equipment, and a miniature train running to the stockyards.

The museum highlights industries from the town's early days, such as the Cedar Lake Handle Factory that was established in 1870. It made wooden handles for potato mashers, rolling pins, and agricultural tools that it shipped as far as Europe.

1955 WHITING STANDARD OIL REFINERY EXPLOSION

Where can you learn about a massive explosion that blotted out the sky and wiped out a whole neighborhood?

The Whiting-Robertsdale Historical Society Museum chronicles the history of the lakefront town known for Pierogi Fest and for refining much of the Midwest's gasoline. A dark chapter was the 1955 Standard Oil Refinery explosion that blackened the dawn sky and wiped the Stiglitz Park neighborhood off the map, forcing about 700 people out of their homes. Billowing plumes of thick smoke reached a mile high and there rose a tower of fire that could be seen 60 miles away. One bystander said it "seemed like the end of the world," telling *The Times of Northwest Indiana*, "I thought the sun exploded."

Hundreds were evacuated after shrapnel from the hydroformer rained down on the city, including a 180-ton chunk of steel that smashed a neighborhood grocery store. The heat melted train cars and the force of the blast flipped automobiles. It was felt as far away as Michigan. The blast blew out every window for miles, so when everyone rushed out of bed barefoot to see what happened, people all over town suffered cuts on their feet from broken glass. The roaring inferno raged for eight days, burning up millions of gallons of gasoline.

The museum, which is open on Sunday afternoons, offers a wealth of information about local history, including streetcars, the J.J. Newberry fire, the giant Falstaff beer cans on the nearby Chicago Skyway, and the shoreline's great alewife invasion.

The Whiting-Robertsdale Historical Society Museum charts the history of the Standard Oil Refinery.

WHITING-ROBERTSDALE HISTORICAL SOCIETY MUSEUM

WHAT: Repository of Standard Oil Refinery history

WHERE: 1610 119th St., Whiting, IN

COST: Free

PRO TIP: Check out the nearby Mascot Hall of Fame, a two-story multimillion-dollar tribute to professional and collegiate mascots whose facade features the biggest booger you ever saw.

The National Guard was called in, and rumors swirled that they shot oil tanks to relieve pressure so they wouldn't explode. Miraculously, only two people died in the massive explosion: a foreman who suffered a heart attack (a week before retirement) and a boy killed with shrapnel in his bedroom. You can learn more at the museum, which has exhibits about the refinery, the high school, town churches, and the White Castle restaurant. You can grab a copy of *One Minute After Sunrise*, John Hmurovic's excellent book about the disaster. "Everyone knew where they were or what they were doing when it happened," he told *The Times*. "It was like when President Kennedy was assassinated. Everyone vividly remembers when it happened."

PINHOOK BOG IN INDIANA DUNES NATIONAL PARK

Where can you walk on water and watch plants eat bugs?

Carnivorous plants akin to but more extravagant than the Venus Fly Trap wait for prey at the Indiana Dunes National Park's Pinhook Bog, a remnant of that last ice age with such a unique and fragile ecosystem that people can only visit on a National Park Service Ranger–led tour on weekends during the summer. While trekking along the Pinhook Bog trails, you can see carnivorous pitcher plants, carnivorous sundew plants, and many rare orchids, including pink lady's slipper orchids. Visit Indiana declared it one of Indiana's must-see natural wonders.

It features two trails: The 2.1-mile packed-dirt Upland Trail wends through a thick forest atop a glacial moraine that dates back 15,000 years, taking you up to ridgelines overlooking a vast valley. A footbridge gives a sweeping view of the bog carved out by the glacier. A green mat of floating peat moss coats the still waters surrounded by serene woodlands. While the Upland Trail can be traversed by the public at any time, the 0.9-mile Bog Trail is restricted.

Guided tours lead hikers to where a large piece of ice broke off the melting glacier, causing a depression in the moraine that

PINHOOK BOG

WHAT: Prehistoric bog home to many carnivorous plants

WHERE: 946 N Wozniak Rd., La Porte, IN

COST: Free

PRO TIP: Make sure to make an appointment in order to get full access to the site.

Pinhook Bog is coated with floating peat moss.

resulted in the bog. You can walk over the wetlands on a section of floating boardwalk right at water level. The rare plants are a sight to behold. The pitcher plants have heavily veined green or red leaves that are folded into a pitcher shape—hence the name!— that's often partly filled with water. Unsuspecting insects land on the inviting lips that flare out only to be dissolved in enzymes and converted into nitrogen. The smaller round-leaved sundews have sticky leaves that trap bugs. Visitors also can see the fuzzy petals of bog buckbean, the green-veined white grass-of-Parnassus flowers, and orange-fringed orchids protruding from the bog. Author Glenda Daniel noted that the wildflowers here are "more delicate-looking than hothouse orchids."

The 580-acre National Natural Landmark is one of just a few bogs in Indiana. It's a glacial kettle filled with stagnant, acidic water not fed by any stream or groundwater. The sphagnum moss gets so thick that other plants grow in it.

MEMORIAL OPERA HOUSE IN VALPARAISO

Where did John Philip Sousa and the Marx Brothers once take the stage?

Big names once performed at The Memorial Opera House in downtown Valparaiso. The 364-seat auditorium is a historic, Queen Anne–style, Grand Army of the Republic memorial hall, which was built in 1893 to honor Porter County's Civil War veterans. An impressive list of performers has taken the stage in the hallowed hall, including bandleader John Philip Sousa, President Theodore Roosevelt, the Marx Brothers, and acclaimed actress Ruth Gordon, who was just a Tony Award short of an EGOT, though she was nominated for her leading role in *The Matchmaker*.

Today, it's home to plays, lunchtime cabarets, and a concert series that brings The Four Seasons, The Beatles, and Pink Floyd tribute acts to town. Proceeds help fund the restoration of the historic performing arts venue that was built after Civil War veteran J.R. Drapier delivered a rousing speech at a Grand Army of the Republic meeting. He declared, "We want to do something for our hometown rather than have the town do something for us," according to the *Vidette-Messenger*. Valpo raised funds with dinners, bake sales, and lecture tickets. The venue hosted plays, concerts, lectures, political rallies, and social gatherings. It was the first theater in Valparaiso to screen movies.

Some notable performers over the years include the mathematical and mind-reading dog Bronte, and Beulah Bondi, who played Jimmy Stewart's mother in *It's a Wonderful Life* and was one of the first to be nominated for the Best Supporting Actress Academy Award. It hosted Prof. Wm. McCormick, billed as a "whistling imitator, magician, and ventriloquist." Several renovations have taken place over the years, including replacing

The Memorial Opera House has been entertaining Valparaiso since the 19th century.

the seats with those from the defunct Star Plaza Theatre in Merrillville. Preservationists hope to keep it around for future generations. "We're such a disposable society," Executive Director Scot MacDonald told *The Times of Northwest Indiana*.

MEMORIAL OPERA HOUSE

WHAT: Historic music venue

WHERE: 104 Indiana Ave., Valparaiso, IN

COST: Tickets vary in price

PRO TIP: Make sure to dine at one of the many celebrated restaurants in downtown Valparaiso, such as Don Quijote, Furin Japanese Restaurant & Bar, Pikk's Tavern, Stacks, or Lincoln Flats.

Yesteryear Is Just Around the Corner author Robert Flood noted that the Memorial Opera House is "not big but cozy," "has been described as having the feel of a small Ford Theatre," and "takes you back in time."

161

HOMELESS JESUS AT VALPARAISO UNIVERSITY

How does this sculpture aim to provoke more empathy for the plight of others?

The universe can be a cold, uncaring place and people even more callous. A sculpture on the Valparaiso University campus aims to change that. The Brauer Museum of Art at the private Lutheran liberal arts school installed the life-sized *Homeless Jesus* sculpture on a bench by Harre Union in 2015 to encourage people to be more compassionate toward the plight of others. Canadian sculptor Timothy P. Schmalz came up with the idea of a homeless Jesus laying on a park bench, shrouded under a blanket. The stigmata wounds on his feet are the only suggestion that it's the messiah of the Christian faith, exhorting people to take a closer look at those they are conditioned to pass by without noticing.

The piece is meant to suggest that Christ is to be counted among the most marginalized in a visual representation of Matthew 25. Though the figure is the size of an adult man, the sculpture leaves room for people to share the bench in contemplative reflection, perhaps on how society casts aside so many people with little regard for their well-being. Schmalz, who hails from Ontario, is known for his religious art. He was inspired after seeing a homeless man sleeping on a park bench in Toronto

The Homeless Jesus *sculpture at Valparaiso University aims to prompt people to think about the less fortunate.*

and realizing that it could just as easily be Jesus. He installed the first *Homeless Jesus* sculpture in Toronto in 2013, got the pope's blessing, and has since installed similar pieces in London, Austria, and across the United States. Then-curator Gregg Hertzlieb of the Brauer Museum of Art told *The Times of Northwest Indiana* that he hopes the piece will spark conversation: "It is a complex work that reminds the campus community of spirituality and moving themes that lie at the heart of the university's mission."

Another notable sculpture nearby is the Italian sculptor Sergio Furnari's *Lunchtime on Top of a Skyscraper*, a bronze version of the iconic construction site photo that was displayed at 9/11's Ground Zero and toured the country before finding a home outside the Industrial Revolution restaurant.

MIDWEST RAIL RANGER HISTORY TOUR

When does a train ride include local history lessons?

You can hop on the South Shore Line, the more-than-century-old commuter rail line to Chicago, and learn a bit about local history. The Midwest Rail Rangers offer periodic educational classes to train riders on the electrified South Shore Line that runs from South Bend through Chicago, taking many commuters from the Calumet Region into The City, as it's called in the local parlance. Interpretive guides give free history lessons to the public about Chicago trivia, Northwest Indiana's steel mills, the Indiana Dunes, and the breadbasket in La Porte and St. Joseph counties. There are multiple stops where people can hop on and board the designated car where the narration takes place. Yellow signs direct riders to the nonprofit's programming, which usually happens near the middle of the train. A schedule is posted online.

The programs are typically reserved for less busy trains so they're not interfering with anyone's trip, be it for work or leisure. No advance registration is needed or taken. You just have to have a South Shore Line pass or buy a ticket, which can be done at any train station. The seats are taken on a first-come, first-served basis. Since 2017, the Wisconsin-based Midwest Rail Rangers have provided these live onboard educational programs

For a schedule of upcoming programs or more information, visit railrangers.org. You have to get train tickets separately but they can be purchased at any station or even on-board the train when the ticket-taker makes his rounds.

The South Shore Line commuter train periodically hosts Midwest Rail Ranger history tours.

MIDWEST RAIL RANGERS TOUR

WHAT: Historical tours on South Shore Line trains

WHERE: Any South Shore Line station

COST: One-way tickets range from $6.25 to $14.25, and a $1 service charge is added if purchased on the train

PRO TIP: Try to get there early to get a good seat.

to teach travelers "about the people, places, and things outside their windows" on trains across the Upper Midwest, including on the South Shore Line. It typically hosts lectures on Thursdays, Saturdays, and Sundays a few times a month. The group also has put out a dozen rail guidebooks and given lectures at local libraries on the history of the South Shore Line, the last interurban train left running in the country.

KINGSBURY ORDNANCE PLANT IN LA PORTE

Where are the remnants of one of World War II's biggest ordnance plants?

The Region was home to the Aetna Powder Works dynamite factory and World War II–era tank plants in East Chicago and Hammond, where a row of tanks once lined 165th Street outside the old Pullman factory. But no munitions or military plant was more prominent than Kingsbury Ordnance Plant, which author Jonathan W. Thomas described as an "engine of war for a brief period in the 1940s." It was in fact one of the world's largest munitions factories during World War II. The plant was near enough to Lake Michigan and the rail lines to ship the weapons and ammunition out to the front lines but remote enough to be safe from enemy bombardment, encompassing 13,000 acres in a largely rural area. The factory drew thousands of workers—many of whom were women (think: Rosie the Riveter)—to La Porte County. It employed more than 21,000 workers in the company town of Kingsford Heights, which was shrouded in secrecy to keep it safe from foreign intelligence. The complex consisted of dozens of factories, warehouses, and machine shops. It was like a self-sustaining town, equipped with infrastructure like water towers, rail lines, and canteens. Workers forged the bullets and bombs deployed on the European and Pacific fronts.

KINGSBURY ORDNANCE PLANT

WHAT: World War II munitions factory

WHERE: 3802 Hupp Rd., La Porte, IN

COST: Free

PRO TIP: Be aware that some areas of the sprawling former plant are private and no longer open to the public.

Top: *Much of the historic Kingsbury Ordnance Plant is now closed off to the public.*

Inset: *The Kingsbury Ordnance Plant was built to supply the front lines during World War II.*

Kingsbury Ordnance was revived for a short time during the Korean War and then forsaken like so many blighted structures in the Region's industrial towns. It's been vacant since the 1960s. Businesses repurposed some of the structures. Part of the area was turned into the Kingsbury Fish and Wildlife Area, a recreational destination for outdoorsmen. But most of the abandoned buildings have been left exposed to the elements. "Other, less useful buildings have been left to rot and are falling down, leading to the picture of a post-apocalyptic wasteland," Thomas wrote. "You could film *The Walking Dead* here and not need to dress the set."

There's nothing to stop someone from wandering around the remote rural ruins Thomas described as a "scarred landscape... with a harsh beauty to it." He wrote, "These ghostly bunkers, a remnant of a war long gone, sit there, abandoned in the landscape."

ELECTRIC CAR PROTOTYPE AT LA PORTE HISTORICAL SOCIETY MUSEUM

Can you picture an orthodontist driving one of the earliest electric cars around town?

Teslas and other electric cars now crisscross roads all over the country. But when La Porte orthodontist Dr. Harold D. Kesling designed the fully electric Yare in the 1970s, the pioneering car was ahead of its time. The bright yellow fiberglass vehicle, pointed at both ends, must have been quite eye-catching when he drove it around town. Its avant-garde look is best described as a mix between a Boxcar Racer and an experimental vehicle racing across the Bonneville Salt Flats (though the Yare only topped out at 55 mph). Kesling, also credited with dentistry advances like a device for correcting crooked teeth, was inspired by his own father and uncles, who devised the Pony-Go carriage propelled by dangling carrots ahead of a horse.

His 72-volt Yare with a range of 50 miles is displayed at the La Porte Historical Society Museum along with his son Dr. Peter C. Kesling's automotive collection of dozens of rare and vintage cars that include a 1930 Delage, a 1934 Citroen, and

Named for a nautical term meaning "ready," the Yare was exhibited at the 1977 Electric Vehicle Exhibition in Chicago's McCormick Place. It was powered by 12 lead acid batteries and given a streamlined contour to make it easy to maneuver.

Left: *The Yare was a 1970s prototype for an electric car.*

Right: *The DeLorean at the La Porte Historical Society Museum will take you back to the future.*

DR. HAROLD D. KESLING'S YARE AND THE KESLING AUTOMOTIVE COLLECTION

WHAT: Experimental 1970s electric car

WHERE: La Porte Historical Society Museum at 2405 Indiana Ave. #1, La Porte, IN

COST: $5

PRO TIP: Budget plenty of time to visit the massive three-story museum, which is much larger and more comprehensive than many local history museums in the area.

a DeLorean. His love of vehicles dated back to his purchase of a 1925 Model T Ford at the age of 14 and led him to make a 6,000-mile transcontinental trip in a 1903 Winton. He collected many cars—often buying them without bumpers, seats, or tires—and restored them to mint condition. Peter Kesling founded Door Prairie Auto Museum near the landmark, nine-sided, 19th-century Door Prairie Barn, where he displayed his car collection, including the 1948 Tucker Torpedo Jeff Bridges drove in the movie *Tucker*. He ended up selling the three-story, 30,000 square-foot Greek Revival building to the La Porte County Historical Society, where more than 10,000 artifacts are now exhibited. You can see parts of historic buildings Kesling salvaged, the Giese Chapel, and a replica of the clock tower at a courthouse designed by Chicago's first professional architect.

JOSEPHUS WOLF HOUSE

Where can you tour a 19th-century mansion that's been home to monks, brides, and the homeless?

The 19th century Josephus Wolf House, a stately Victorian Italianate mansion, was built by a pioneer settler of Portage Township whom the *Chesterton Tribune* described as "one of Porter County's history makers." The Ohio native settled in a prairie in what was then wilderness and is credited with its development. After striking it rich during the California Gold Rush, he became a major landholder who established a 5,000-acre farm that has been compared to "a miniature city, covered as it was with fine barns and a magnificent farm home." He had nearly 350 head of cattle that he raised for the nearby Chicago Stockyards. Wolf's towering three-story mansion, whose cupola affords a view of the Chicago skyline on a clear day, has cycled through many different uses over the years. The 7,800-square-foot home has been a bridal shop, an antique store, a woman's homeless shelter, and a Franciscan monastery of the Seven Dolors Shrine.

> ### JOSEPHUS WOLF HOUSE
>
> ---
>
> **WHAT:** Historic mansion built by early settler
>
> **WHERE:** 453 W 700 N, Portage, IN
>
> **COST:** Free
>
> **PRO TIP:** Call 219-364-8102 to arrange for a tour.

The 18-room house was originally built in 1875 as the center of a family farm where livestock and dairy cows were raised. You can arrange for tours to see the great room, parlor, study, library, and main hall with a walnut staircase. The historic house features pine molding, red oak floors, Indiana limestone, a massive porch, and some artistic flourishes like carvings of fruit in the front door. German bricklayers built this house that's listed on the National Register of Historic Places. It's rumored

Top: *The Josephus Wolf House was built by one of Porter Township's early pioneers.*

Inset: *The 18-room Josephus Wolf House is listed on the National Register of Historic Places.*

to have possibly been a stop on the Underground Railroad and also to be haunted. You can learn more in the Portage Community Historical Society in Countryside Park or on the historical displays on brick pillars in Founders Square, a park now surrounded with shiny new modern apartments amid a mixed-use development at the heart of the Porter County suburb that dates back to 1959.

Josephus Wolf, who raised both prime beef cattle and dairy cows, accumulated his land over time. He was renowned for his hospitality and for never letting a visitor leave his estate hungry.

ST. ANDREW THE APOSTLE CHURCH IN CALUMET CITY

When is a cathedral not technically a cathedral?

Though not officially a cathedral, St. Andrew the Apostle Church in Calumet City sure seems like one. The towering Catholic church wows with spectacular visuals, including the ornate organ and 20-foot-tall stained glass windows crafted in Munich that represent the 15 Mysteries of the Rosary. Its opulent splendor owes a lot to the extensive use of marble quarried by workmen in Pietrasanta, Italy. Described as "the ultimate in craftsmanship," the sanctuary showcases lustrous slabs of marble that can display more than a dozen shades, colors, and textures in a single piece. The church of St. Andrew the Apostle wasn't always so resplendent. It was founded in 1891 as the first Catholic Church in Cal City, which early Polish settlers originally called Sobieski Park. A tornado destroyed the church the next year. Parishioners began rebuilding with brick and lumber recovered from the ruined frame structure. The church was again razed by fire in 1918. Services were held in the basement of the church school until the current church was constructed in 1930.

Architects Sandel & Strong designed the grandiose Romanesque building that was crafted by laborers from Germany, Belgium, France, and Italy. As the parish website puts it, "On your first visit to St. Andrew, you will no doubt be amazed at the beauty and craftsmanship of the church." Take for instance the statue of Mary teaching the multitudes on the south side of the sanctuary, described as the "only one of its kind in the Western Hemisphere," or the statue of St. Joseph carrying a thin blade of polished marble. The huge Poor Souls

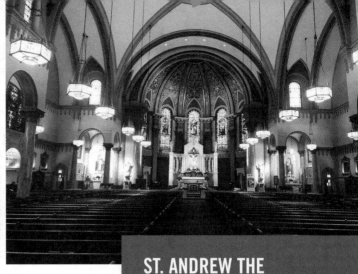

Left: *St. Andrew the Apostle was built with marble imported from Europe.*

Right: *The extravagant church is filled with statuary.*

ST. ANDREW THE APOSTLE

WHAT: Church that looks like a cathedral

WHERE: 768 Lincoln Ave., Calumet City, IL

COST: Free

PRO TIP: Be sure to check out the portrait of the Black Madonna of Poland and the St. Andrew the Apostle shrine that shows the patron saint of the parish with his signature X-shaped cross.

in Purgatory shrine, copied from a statue in Spain, was carved of marble quarried in Belgium. The intricate piece depicts Christ in the tomb beneath a marble altar. Everywhere you turn in the grandiose church, there's an artistic rendering of scripture for inspiration.

The parish was consolidated with Our Lady of Knock and St. Victor in Calumet City by the Archdiocese of Chicago to make the churches more sustainable for the long term. It's now part of the Jesus, Shepherd of Souls parish.

CHICAGO AIR AND WATER SHOW STAGING GROUNDS

Where can you see Blue Angels roaring off into the sky?

The Chicago Air and Water Show is a love-it-or-hate-it affair. Many Chicagoans grumble and grouse when supersonic planes roar overhead all weekend. It's loud and disruptive. Militaristic pomp and ceremony are not everyone's cup of jet fuel. But the event's popularity is undeniable with an estimated 400,000 visitors lining the city's beaches. The Blue Angels and other military jets stage in Gary, which used to have an air show of its own—the bygone South Shore Air Show—that got put on hiatus indefinitely as a result of the Steel City's budget woes and no major sponsors stepping up. Photographers love to set up outside the Gary/Chicago International Airport to shoot startlingly close-up photos of the Navy and Air Force planes as they take off and land. Finding a perch just outside the airport, which serves mainly as a logistics hub after never really taking off as a commercial airport, affords a much more intimate view of the fighter jets than you can see from a beach along Chicago's Lake Michigan shore. It's like going to a black box theater instead of Broadway.

Hundreds of photographers, aviation buffs, and military veterans gather along Airport Road at the end of Runway 30

CHICAGO AIR AND WATER SHOW STAGING

WHAT: Where the planes take off and land

WHERE: Gary/Chicago International Airport at 6001 Airport Rd., Gary, IN

COST: Free

PRO TIP: Show up early, scout out a good spot, and bring a high-powered lens.

People park outside the Gary Airport to watch the fighter jets take off for the Chicago Air and Water Show.

to take in the spectacle every summer. You can watch the planes return in formation and execute a carrier break where they peel away from the formation one after the other to land individually. Professional photographer and filmmaker Guy Rhodes, who's covered a few Olympic Games, goes there to photograph the Blue Angels and other planes "because you don't have to fight the crowds downtown, mainly." "When the Blue Angels come in to land, they'll typically execute a 'carrier break' for landing, which is pretty dramatic," he said. "So, in a way, you get a little 60-second show with very little hassle."

The South Shore Convention and Visitors Authority Board has been in talks with the city of Gary about potentially bringing food trucks and other festivities since hundreds of people turn out every year with almost no publicity.

HIDDEN FISHING PIER AT AN INTERNATIONAL PORT

Where can you fish across a channel from one of the largest steel mills in the United States?

Northwest Indiana has 45 miles of coastline along Lake Michigan, two-thirds of which has been developed. While the Great Lake appears as vast as an ocean from the shore, it's hardly like visiting Fort Lauderdale, Myrtle Beach, or some other touristy getaway. Almost every beach has a view of a steel mill, oil refinery, or power plant. You can never escape the ever-present backdrop of the Rust Belt's heavy industry as noted by a *New York Times* article with the headline "Welcome to America's Newest National Park. Don't Mind the Power Plant." Despite all the smoke-belching factories, Northwest Indiana remains an outdoorsman's paradise where glaciers carved out the many lakes where fishermen can catch trout, bluegill, and salmon—the biggest being Lake Michigan.

While you can launch a boat from various marinas, the Great Lake has relatively few sites where you can fish from the shore. Most are clustered along the lakefront and Trail Creek in Michigan City. But there's a public fishing pier run

The Marquette Plan championed by Congressman Pete Visclosky would reclaim the lakefront for parkland as it deindustrializes. A steel waste processing plant was recently turned into the Indiana Dunes National Park's Portage Lakefront and Riverwalk, which also has a fishing pier.

There's a hidden public fishing pier at the Port of Indiana-Burns Harbor across from one of the nation's largest steel mills.

PUBLIC FISHING PIER

WHAT: Hidden fishing spot at an international port

WHERE: Northeast corner of the Port of Indiana-Burns Harbor at 6635 S Boundary Rd., Portage, IN

COST: Free

PRO TIP: The port has restricted access but all you have to do to get in is have a fishing license and flash a driver's license or ID at the gate.

by the Indiana Department of Natural Resources where the Burns Waterway flows into Lake Michigan to a spot that's about as secret they get: at the far northeast corner of the Port of Indiana-Burns Harbor. The public fishing pier for shoreline anglers sits across a channel from the hulking Cleveland-Cliffs Burns Harbor steel mill. The massive integrated mill is so big it makes the train cars and cranes in the foreground look like toys. It's almost a surreal spot for fishing. The water remains bright blue and crystal clear despite the piles of iron ore and limestone that looms off in the background, where towering blast furnaces forge iron with cauldron-like heat that's been compared to hell itself. You might want to catch and release since the mills are allowed to discharge arsenic, hexavalent chromium, and other chemicals into Lake Michigan.

HOOSIER VALLEY RAILROAD MUSEUM

Where can you learn hobo signs and ride the rails?

The Hoosier Valley Railroad Museum in North Judson sits along a historic railroad line and gives visitors a chance to ride the rail, offering short train trips every weekend that cross over a bridge spanning the Kankakee River. The museum is filled with a wealth of history about railroads like the Monon, the Erie Lackawanna, Amtrak, and the South Shore Line. You can enter exhibit-stuffed train cars, including a Pullman Sleeper that carried troops off to World War II. Described by Museum President Todd Flanigan as a "must-see tourist destination" that promotes Region rail history, it's filled with memorabilia like uniforms, ticket booths, and railroad equipment. There's a visual dictionary of the signs hobos used to communicate with each other while riding the rails. The curators also have a sense of humor with photo captions repeatedly referring to unidentified "things" being pictured and a random insertion of Garfield that says "this has nothing to do with railroads but who doesn't love Garfield."

It's all aboard for 10-mile round-trip train rides along a short line between North Judson and English Lake every Saturday during the summer. The Hoosier Valley Railroad Museum also runs seasonal Santa Trains, Halloween Trains, and Pumpkin Trains where you can behold the glory of the countryside's fall foliage. It recently added an extensively

You can ride in authentic railroad cabooses or open-air sightseeing railcars to soak in more of the picturesque rural landscape. It's best to reserve tickets in advance as seats are limited.

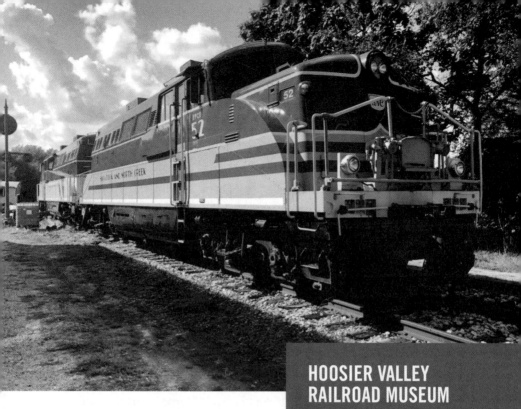

One can ride the train at the Hoosier Valley Railroad Museum.

renovated Bock Lumber Co. No. 1 steam locomotive that museum treasurer Robert Barcus said looks like "something you would normally only find in a storybook." The museum celebrates a bygone era of train travel, giving people the opportunity to experience first-hand "the sights, sounds, and smells of post-World War II railroading." The rides provide a pleasant immersion into what it was like to be a passenger waiting at the train station or aboard a railcar, as well as what railroad workers in depots, dispatch centers, and crossing shacks experienced.

HOOSIER VALLEY RAILROAD MUSEUM

WHAT: Train museum

WHERE: 507 Mulberry St., North Judson, IN

COST: Free, but donations encouraged and $10 for a train ride

PRO TIP: While in town, swing by the Works Progress Administration built Norwayne Field park and the vintage Point drive-in, at least to snap photos of the giant soft-serve ice cream cone.

NO-CAN-DO POND AT SUNSET HILL FARM PARK

Why can't you do anything at this pond?

The No-Can-Do Pond at Sunset Hill Farm Park just north of Valparaiso has an unusual name. There's a backstory: Farmers dug the pond in 1952 to be able to draw water to fight fires if needed. Since it was artificially constructed, they banned boating, fishing, swimming, skating, and basically any recreational activities—hence "no can do." Fortunately, today there's plenty to do at the sprawling county park. Sunset Hill Farm is home to barns full of antique historic farm equipment, goats and other farm animals, a model railroad garden, a working agricultural garden, a children's education center, seas of prairie, woods for hiking, and an annual summer music festival. One of the coolest features is the children's storytime trail installed by the Porter County Public Library System. You can read a children's book posted on signs a few pages at a time while making their way along a mile-long trail filled with varied scenery. It's also a great place for bird watching.

The 235-acre farm at US 6 and Meridian Road in Liberty Township was once owned by Chicago businessman Col. Robert Murray, who built a white frame house there in the 1930s and sold eggs and milk out of the big barn. The milk business was a big hit in the area but was discontinued in

NO-CAN-DO POND AT SUNSET HILL FARM PARK

WHAT: Unusually named pond at dairy farm-turned-county park that showcases agricultural practices

WHERE: 775 Meridian Rd., Valparaiso, IN

COST: Free

PRO TIP: The hiking is excellent at the park but what sets it apart is all the vintage farm equipment and farm animals.

Pretty much nothing is allowed at the No-Can-Do Pond at Sunset Hill Farm Park.

the 1970s after the owners signed a deal to sell milk to Dixie Dairy. The farm was left to Purdue University "for the benefit of agriculture" but was eventually turned over to Porter County and preserved as a park. Barns and silos remain among new structures like playgrounds, the naturalist's office, and an interpretive center. The colonel's wife, Sue Murray, "a very exacting person" who oversaw the grounds, established the rules for the No-Can-Do Pond, bestowing the picturesque body of water with an unforgettable name.

Sunset Hill was known as "the big poultry farm owned by the Chicago millionaire." Its Guernsey cows produced milk so rich you couldn't see a nickel in the bottom of a milk bucket with only an inch left in the pail.

PULLMAN NATIONAL MONUMENT

Where did Labor Day originate?

The Calumet Region is filled with company towns. Hammond was built around a slaughterhouse, Whiting a refinery, and Gary and East Chicago around steel mills. One East Chicago neighborhood, Marktown, was created by industrialist Clayton Mark as a replica of a Swiss village where workers could walk across the street to the Mark Manufacturing Company. Famed architect Howard Van Doren Shaw designed the planned worker community where residents parked on the sidewalks and walked on the streets, and which was named one of the "Seven Wonders of Northwest Indiana." You can tour the neighborhood that's listed on the National Register of Historic Places, but it has lost some of its homes and all of its stores over the years.

The gold standard for historic preservation of planned worker communities in the area is South Side Chicago's Pullman neighborhood. The company town where workers built luxury train cars that once crisscrossed the country was named a National Monument in 2015, got $34 million in renovations, and turned the Pullman factory's historic Administration Clock Tower building into a visitors center. You can stroll around the factory grounds to see a railway garden, a restored worker's gate, and many informative signs

---

Every October, residents of Pullman welcome visitors inside their abodes for the Pullman Home Tour. The chance to peek inside historic homes is the largest annual fundraiser for the Pullman Historic Foundation, which maintains a museum on the site.

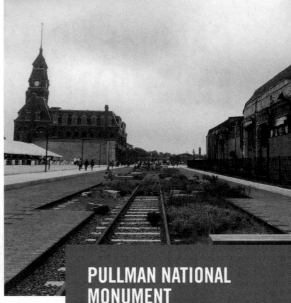

Left: *The historic Administration Clock Tower Building is now home to the Pullman National Monument's Visitor Center.*

Right: *One can stroll along a new railroad garden at an old railroad factory.*

PULLMAN NATIONAL MONUMENT

WHAT: Planned worker community where Labor Day originated

WHERE: 610 E 111th St., Chicago, IL

COST: Free

PRO TIP: Walk around the neighborhood to soak in the residential architecture. The National A. Philip Randolph Pullman Porter Museum at 10406 S Maryland Ave. is a bit of a trek but an underappreciated gem that tells the workers' story.

shining light on the historical significance of the town. You can learn about industrialist George Pullman's Pullman Palace Car Co. and its role in the history of organized labor, including the 1937 contract the African-American Brotherhood of Sleeping Car Porters secured with the company and 1894 strike Pullman incited by cutting wages while maintaining high rents. The strike paralyzed the national railway system—then the main way people got around—and was crushed by the federal government, leading President Grover Cleveland to declare Labor Day a holiday in a reconciliation bid. You can learn about Pullman's impact from exhibits concerning labor rights, civil rights, urban planning, and the industrial revolution.

CALUMET CITY SMILEY FACE WATER TOWERS

Why are the iconic water towers always smiling?

The audience at the River Oaks Theater at the River Oaks mall in Calumet City reportedly started gasping, cheering, laughing, and even fleeing from the theater during a screening of *The Silence of the Lambs* when it was mentioned that serial killer Buffalo Bill might be hiding out in Cal City. The south suburban Chicago community hugging the state line, originally known as West Hammond, also takes pride that its iconic Smiley Face Water Towers were featured in Oliver Stone's *Natural Born Killers*. The city has long had a reputation as a Sin City known for its go-go dancers, night clubs, and mob ties.

It sought to paint itself in a more positive light in 1973 when Kim Forero, then an 8-year-old girl, wrote a letter saying smiley faces would make the water towers look cute. Her heartfelt plea persuaded city officials to commission Chicago Bridge & Iron Co. to paint the million-gallon water towers lemon-yellow and add huge "have-a-nice-day" smiles like those often seen on restaurant takeout bags. Mr. and Mrs. Smiley became instant icons and symbols of the city, grinning down on everyone. They've been plastered on bumper stickers, emblazoned on T-shirts, and displayed on miniature scale models all around town.

SMILEY FACE TOWERS

WHAT: Cal City's sunniest landmarks

WHERE: Almost anywhere in Cal City

COST: Free

PRO TIP: Swing by the Calumet City Historical Society at 760 Wentworth Ave. to learn more about the city's history, which sadly does not include the "Calumet City Egg Donation Center and House of Blues" mentioned in *30 Rock*.

Left: *The Lincoln Funeral Train entered Illinois in Calumet City.*

Right: *A water tower model smiles at the Calumet City Historical Society Museum.*

The giant water towers are a ubiquitous sight in Calumet City given their massive size.

Other points of interest in the city include the Calumet City Historical Society and the historic marker at State Line Road and State Street that notes the Lincoln Funeral Train first entered Illinois along the railroad tracks just north of there. The museum hosts regular author talks and has many exhibits about the community's history, including its Catholic churches, Polish heritage, and bygone businesses. Fun fact: The hamburger press was invented in Calumet City, making the shaping of ground beef into burger patties an assembly line process.

Mr. Smiley by the River Oaks mall sports a bow tie. Mrs. Smiley is painted pink. The couple inspired many copycats. Cal City kept them even after the smiley faces commonly seen on buttons during the 1970s faded in popularity.

COFFEE CREEK WATERSHED NATURE PRESERVE

Where can you find wilderness at the edge of neatly manicured suburban lawns?

Northwest Indiana is home to the Calumet Rivers, the Kankakee River, many inland lakes carved out by glaciers, and of course Lake Michigan. But one of the Region's gems of pristine nature runs along a simple stream. You can hike over boardwalks amid seas of prairie and bright yellow wildflowers at the Coffee Creek Watershed Nature Preserve. It's a 157-acre complex of wetlands, woodland, and prairies where more than 400 native plant species have been identified. Tucked between Chesterton and Valparaiso, it's surrounded by suburbanization, including single-family homes, senior housing, offices, and restaurants. But it's an oasis where hikes lead through lush green forests, rustling prairies, and wetlands. Boardwalks extend over marshes and swales, while seven bridges take walkers and runners over the gently flowing Coffee Creek that runs 2.5 miles through the park. Salmon and trout spawn there before heading off to Lake Michigan.

In the spring and fall, you also can break out the binoculars and spot an array of migratory birds funneled

COFFEE CREEK WATERSHED NATURE PRESERVE

WHAT: Natural oasis nestled in suburbia

WHERE: 2401 Village Pt., Chesterton, IN

COST: Free

PRO TIP: Grab a map to find your way around as many boardwalks have been closed for repairs.

You can explore more than 150 acres at the Coffee Creek Watershed Preserve.

by Lake Michigan to Northwest Indiana along with indigenous bluebirds, sparrows, warblers, red-tailed hawks, bald eagles, and ospreys or fish hawks while hiking along the five miles of trails. Conservationists installed nesting platforms across the nature preserve to conserve the ospreys whose numbers were greatly reduced because of past pesticide use. Ospreys return to the nests every spring, mating for life and hatching two to four chicks a year. Watching the raptors hunt is a sight to behold as they dive feet-first with their sharp talons extended and rise up with fish. Whitetail deer and other wildlife also can be spotted at the park. Amid the wild, untrammeled nature, there's also the Chesterton Amphitheater with a sweeping pond view and the massive 3,600-acre pavilion with 20 picnic tables in a tree-circled meadow.

There's something different to see every season. The bird watching and fish spawning peak in the spring and fall. The summer is the time to bear witness to what's been described as a "magnificent display of wildflowers."

SCHRAGE MANSION AND LOURDES GROTTO

Where can you see a grotto modeled after the one in Lourdes, France?

Everyone in Whiting should know where the Schrage Mansion is located. The stately abode was built in 1897 in Whiting by German immigrant Henry Schrage, who played an outsized role in the development of the lakefront city. The Civil War veteran was one of the first to settle the swampy area just off Lake Michigan. Schrage opened the first store, became the first postmaster, and arranged the deal that let Standard Oil build a refinery in a frontier town where people brawled on the street. In 1895, he founded the First Bank of Whiting that would go on to become Centier, a multibillion-dollar behemoth that is now Indiana's largest privately owned bank. Like Strack & Van Til and Schoop's Hamburgers, Centier grew into one of Northwest Indiana's most successful homegrown companies. As his fortunes grew, Schrage also built a large mansion blending the Queen Anne and Romanesque architectural styles on an estate-like setting smack dab in the middle of a far more densely packed urban neighborhood.

In 1928, next door to the Schrage estate, the Immaculate Conception Church built an exact replica of the Lourdes Grotto

Left: *The founder of the bank that would become Centier built the Schrage Mansion in Whiting.*

Right: *The grounds of the Schrage Mansion are well-tended.*

Inset: *The Immaculate Conception Grotto in Whiting is modeled after Lourdes.*

in France where Catholics believe Mary appeared to St. Bernadette in 1858. Today, you can observe a contemplative moment at the grotto crafted with Lake Superior limestone while visiting the Schrage House grounds, which feature an immaculate lawn, garden, fountain, and interpretative signs. The house got listed on the National Register of Historic Places in 2021. The Schrages have been considering doing more to activate the space, possibly tours or a tea room. It's a short walk from the new Centier Corporate History Museum in its longtime downtown Whiting branch at 119th Street. The museum chronicles the bank's more-than-125-year history with historic black-and-white photos, videos, and artifacts like old safes and the stone archway in the door of the original branch.

Urschel Laboratories in Chesterton also has an extensive corporate museum in its lobby that highlights how its cutting machines are used to make bags of shredded lettuce and McDonald's French fries. Unfortunately, it's not open to the public.

A *CHRISTMAS STORY'S* FLICK FOREVER LICKING A FLAGPOLE AT THE INDIANA WELCOME CENTER

Where can you see the flagpole-licking scene from the classic holiday movie?

Hammond's Indiana Welcome Center installed a statue of Flick from *A Christmas Story* licking the frozen flagpole just outside its doors as a photo opportunity for visitors. It's easy to miss while you walk in but many stop there to snap selfies by the bronze dramatization of the Christmas classic's famous scene of Flick being triple-dog dared to make an instantly regrettable decision. The visitor center right off the Borman Expressway is an impressive structure built for $6 million in 1999 with architectural features that celebrate the Region's sand dunes, industry, and agriculture. In its large exhibition hall, it celebrates Hammond native Jean Shepherd with its *Christmas Story* Comes Home exhibit every December. The flagpole sculpture is outside the doors of the center, so it is available for photo ops

INDIANA WELCOME CENTER

WHAT: Where *A Christmas Story*'s Flick forever flicks the flagpole

WHERE: 7770 Corrine Dr., Hammond, IN

COST: Free

PRO TIP: Drop by during one of the many *Christmas Story* Comes Home events, like the mashed potato-eating contest or visits with Jolly Old Saint Nick (played by Shepherd himself in the movie) on Santa Mountain.

Flick licks the flagpole on a triple-dog dare outside the Indiana Welcome Center.

year-round even when the visitor center—known for its art exhibits, short films, many travel brochures, and gift shops—is closed.

You can recreate the classic scene in the movie adaptation of Shepherd's book *In God We Trust: All Others Pay Cash* in which a panicked Flick screams "thstuck... thstuck... thstuck!" Firefighters descend on the school in a scene "that escalated quickly." Now "Flick's stuck forever" at the Indiana Welcome Center, as one headline writer put it. There's also a selfie station inside where you can pose with Ralphie and his trusty old Red Ryder carbine-action, 200-shot, range model air rifle that he's lucky has a compass in the stock. Bring family or friends and have your own *Christmas Story* moment to ring in the holidays Region-style. The gift shop overflows with all things *Christmas Story*, including leg lamps, postcards, toys, refrigerator magnets, shot glasses, socks, bunny outfits, and various other memorabilia. But never forget the true reason for the season: accruing as many likes and shares as possible. Your posted selfie with Flick's tongue stuck to the flagpole should rack up plenty.

The Warren G. Harding Elementary School in Hammond's Hessville neighborhood that's depicted in the movie is not far from the Indiana Welcome Center. But the school was rebuilt and isn't in the same building Shepherd attended and wrote about.

SOURCES

Where John Dillinger Escaped from Jail: Mark Skertic's *A Native's Guide to Northwest Indiana*; https://visitindiana.com/blog/index.php/2013/09/07/visit-the-jailhouse-made-famous-by-john-dillinger; https://www.nwitimes.com/lifestyles/behind-the-bars-beyond-dillinger/article_aa71531e-56b8-5080-830d-93ef8407eb3a.html; https://www.nwitimes.com/news/local/lake/crown-point/volunteers-restore-windows-in-jail-made-famous-by-dillinger-escape/article_3c2ad34c-bd85-57e2-b94a-ed4eec63df41.html.

Diana of the Dunes's Old Stomping Grounds: Jerome Pohlen's *Oddball Indiana*; Alan McPherson's *Nature Walks in the Indiana Dunes*; Glenda Daniel's *Dune Country*; https://www.indianadunes.com/explore-the-dunes/national-park/diana-of-the-dunes-dare; https://www.nwitimes.com/entertainment/indiana-dunes-national-park-offering-diana-of-the-dunes-hikes/article_cea76f0b-535a-5fcc-a9a0-8535b8eecbca.html; https://www.nwitimes.com/business/watch-now-mountains-of-sand-beaches-and-national-park-trails-in-indiana/article_eb015689-1c9a-5eb7-a708-f29359554ef0.html.

Shipwreck at the Bottom of Lake Michigan: *The Wreck of the J.D. Marshall* pamphlet from the Old Lighthouse Museum; https://www.nwitimes.com/news/local/illinois/j-d-marshall-lies-just-offshore-of-indiana-dunes-state-park/article_1e7e1a80-7bdb-5a7b-ad1e-8fd3c70cfc7e.html; https://www.in.gov/dnr/lake-michigan-coastal-program/indiana-shipwrecks/jd-marshall-nature-preserve; https://www.southshorecva.com/blog/post/shipwrecked-in-lake-michigan-jd-marshall.

Submarines Under Lake Michigan: Ray Boomhauer's *Destination Indiana*; Jerome Pohlen's *Oddball Indiana*; http://www.thebeacher.com/pdf/2016/BeacherJan14.pdf; https://mysteriouschicago.com/the-fool-killer-submarine-all-we-know; https://whatsnewlaporte.com/2009/12/27/the-saga-of-the-showboat-dixiana.

Belle Gunness Exhibit: Jerome Pohlen's *Oddball Indiana*; https://www.indystar.com/story/news/history/retroindy/2017/11/10/female-indiana-serial-killer-comely-belle-gunness-loved-her-suitors-death/848023001; https://laportelibrary.org/at-the-library/explore-local/belle-gunness; https://www.legendsofamerica.com/belle-gunness; https://laportecountyhistory.org/exhibits/belle-gunness; https://www.roadsideamerica.com/tip/3465.

Ecology's Birthplace: Alan McPherson's *Nature Walks in the Indiana Dunes*; https://www.lib.uchicago.edu/collex/exhibits/university-chicago-centennial-catalogues/university-chicago-faculty-centennial-view/henry-c-cowles-1869-1939-botany; http://npshistory.com/publications/indu/cook-1999.pdf; https://www.nps.gov/indu/planyourvisit/cb16.htm; https://www.nwitimes.com/2004-legends-inductee-henry-chandler-cowles/article_b154c50f-ff07-503b-9969-4eaa0faa00ef.html.

Mount Baldy: https://www.nps.gov/indu/planyourvisit/mt-baldy.htm; http://www.thebeacher.com/pdf/2015/BeacherMar05.pdf; https://wgnradio.com/chicagos-afternoon-news/mount-baldy-is-alive-and-growing; https://www.smithsonianmag.com/science-nature/mystery-why-dangerous-sand-dune-swallowed-boy-180953404; https://www.nwitimes.com/news/local/mount-baldy-swallowing-parking-lots-exit-road/article_fe995876-8a79-5912-b7d9-a327b1009efb.html.

Tree Graveyards: https://www.indianadunes.com/dunes-101-did-you-know; https://www.nationalgeographic.com/travel/national-parks/article/indiana-dunes-guide-what-to-do; https://www.in.gov/dnr/state-parks/files/dunes_trail.pdf.

Roy Boy's Badlands: https://chicagoreader.com/arts-culture/tiger-king-of-the-midwest; https://www.chicagotribune.com/suburbs/post-tribune/opinion/ct-ptb-davich-roy-boy-cooper-tattoo-st-0202-20180201-story.html; https://www.wbez.org/stories/garys-roy-boy-dies/5996df12-a610-4346-b0c7-ffcaead3152e.

Marriage Mill: https://www.southshorecva.com/blog/post/historic-marriage-mill-returns-to-crown-point/https://www.nwitimes.com/niche/marriage-mill-keeps-crown-points-long-colorful-nuptial-history-alive/article_d25d4ac8-7e8e-52d5-8ff2-daa5c8e98c44.html; https://www.chicagotribune.com/suburbs/post-tribune/ct-ptb-bicentennial-marriage-mill-st-0612-20160610-story.html; https://www.nwitimes.com/news/local/lake/no-run-of-the-mill-marriages-in-crown-point/article_d116628b-b0c5-5ccc-8839-9699c2d56e9d.html.

Indiana Dunes: https://indiananativeplants.org/wp-content/uploads/2020/01/SU16-INPAWS-compressed.pdf; https://www.indianadunes.com/dunes-101-did-you-know.

An Architectural Landmark: https://www.mclib.org/about-us/history; https://www.nwitimes.com/entertainment/late-world-renowned-architect-helmut-jahn-designed-landmarks-in-northwest-indiana-including-the-michigan-city/article_af56b616-f42a-534f-9d41-6f1dd857ff3a.html; https://www.archpaper.com/2021/08/helmut-jahn-life-architecture-is-a-greatest-hits-album-not-an-anthology.

The Great Escape from the Brown Mansion: https://wpl.lib.in.us/westchester-township-history-museum; https://www.youtube.com/watch?v=RgCCJtot5v0; https://www.nwitimes.com/news/special-section/history/organizations/history-keepers-westchester-township-history-museum-and-duneland-historical-society/article_6cc296a1-8175-5900-aa6d-e393ff2a012a.html

Frank Lloyd Wright Homes: https://www.nwitimes.com/news/history/frank-lloyd-wrights-influence-remains-in-nwi-today/article_a1124540-7769-5c72-81ce-73a08074bc9b.html; https://www.nwitimes.com/business/local/historic-frank-lloyd-wright-house-sells-for-more-than-1-million-in-ogden-dunes/article_345cddf8-453f-52bc-96e0-2e5cb9c76395.html.

Nike Missile Bases: https://www.blastcamp.com/history; https://www.nps.gov/articles/nike-missile-site-c47.htm; https://www.indianalandmarks.org/2018/06/tour-cold-war-landmarks-region; https://www.wbez.org/stories/what-happened-to-nike-missile-sites-around-chicago/b09ed69c-cdf0-4382-a7ac-75480a3d4cb7.

A Communion with Craft Beer: https://www.harborcountry-news.com/features/beer-church-to-build-upper-deck-adding-120-outdoor-seats/article_1b94ae24-33fe-5ae7-9140-2d9b378dbd65.html; https://chicago.eater.com/maps/best-michigan-breweries-southwest-road-trip-chicago-beer; https://www.nwitimes.com/business/local/new-buffalo-church-turned-into-brewpub/article_1a442152-c626-54a5-8405-36e21ccbc6a6.html; https://www.nwitimes.com/lifestyles/food-and-cooking/heavenly-hops-19th-century-new-buffalo-church-now-a-taproom-with-more-expansion-to-come/article_02cf157b-a70c-5019-9d39-97d8f9bc4062.html.

Meyer's Castle: https://meyerscastle.com; https://www.nwitimes.com/niche/latest-owner-makes-meyers-castle-her-home-as-well-as-a-regal-place-for-an/article_e520ad14-1bea-518e-a5a5-871e052228d5.html

One of the Most Scenic Trails in America: https://www.nwitimes.com/niche/get-healthy/winter-hikes-are-the-ticket-out-of-the-house-and-into-fun/article_7b36dfde-63cd-5467-bf2b-97a2b468c0f4.html; https://www.indianadunes.com/dunes-101-hiking; https://www.hikingproject.com/trail/7013470/trail-9; https://www.nationalgeographic.com/travel/national-parks/article/indiana-dunes-guide-what-to-do.

Octave Chanute, Grandfather of Flight: Jerome Pohlen's *Oddball Indiana*; https://www.nwitimes.com/uncategorized/calumet-roots-history-starts-to-take-flight-in-region/article_8f851a11-875c-554c-804e-019b7deaba12.html; https://www.nwitimes.com/uncategorized/aquatorium-opening-part-of-8-year-mission/article_e7ea08b3-13f0-5ae2-a35a-62fec6196696.html; https://www.britannica.com/biography/Octave-Chanute; http://memory.loc.gov/master/ipo/qcdata/qcdata/wrightold/wb005.html.

The Frost House, a Temple of 1960s Style: https://thefrosthouse.com; https://www.dwell.com/home/the-frost-house-a02d4a86; https://www.indianalandmarks.org/2018/07/a-modernist-treasure-in-michigan-city.

SS *Eastland* Disaster: https://wsbt.com/news/local/michigan-city-remembers-ss-eastland-disaster-of-1915-with-memorial-service; https://www.southbendtribune.com/story/news/local/2019/07/22/old-lighthouse-museum-to-honor-memory-of-1915-eastland-disaster-victims-saturday/117179416.

Community Veterans Memorial, One of Northwest Indiana's Seven Wonders: http://marktown.org/pdf/marktown-sep07.pdf; https://midwestwanderer.com/community-veterans-memorial-honoring-our-nations-heroes; https://rotblattamrany.com/projects/community-veterans-memorial-park.

Frank Dudley's Duneland: https://news.wttw.com/2015/08/25/look-rare-paintings-indiana-dunes-artist-frank-dudley; https://indianahistory.org/blog/painter-of-the-dunes-a-life-of-frank-virgil-dudley; https://photographyjournal2013.wordpress.com/2013/06/25/frank-v-dudley-studio-cottage-site; https://www.valpo.edu/brauer-museum-of-art/files/2015/01/Paintings.pdf; https://www.nwitimes.com/article_9b76d139-71a7-5ae6-87f2-c0e71febb72a.html.

The Hoosier Slide: https://www.nwitimes.com/uncategorized/dunes-swoon/article_99c1aef1-348d-53e9-a6f1-712948168bd7.html; https://orangebeanindiana.com/2020/01/05/hoosier-slide; https://www.nwitimes.com/business/local/michigan-city-hopes-to-open-lakefront-up-to-public-when-nipsco-plant-decommissioned/article_9158af45-43c8-53c1-833f-b3a285217773.html; https://www.nwitimes.com/news/opinion/columnists/doug-ross/doug-ross-pageant-played-role-in-saving-indiana-dunes/article_ee3d7d7c-7f36-5a09-95f6-a924d77365ca.html; https://www.beachcombingmagazine.com/blogs/news/what-happened-to-hoosier-slide.

The Sparkle House: https://www.nwitimes.com/entertainment/sparkle-house-art-project-to-cover-abandoned-house-in-gary-with-sparkles/article_0f17d88f-909d-510d-b345-49d9cdf849e6.html; www.sparklehouseart.com; https://www.airbnb.com/rooms/39885282?source_impression_id=p3_1632615190_Jc8NNl4v1iH6RlJN&guests=1&adults=1

Southernmost Point of Lake Michigan: https://www.nwitimes.com/news/local/miller-hopes-southern-point-of-lake-michigan-marker-will-boost-tourism/article_10862a4d-ae58-595b-a628-926fb5f20e39.html; http://marquetteparkgary.org/projectdetail.aspx?industry=Natural%20Areas&IGID=12&projectID=33&ProjectName=Lake%20Michigan%20Shoreline.

Cacti in Indiana: https://heinzetrust.org/john-merle-coulter-nature-preserve; https://voices.uchicago.edu/mcart/2021/05/26/eastern-prickly-pear-opuntia-humifusa; https://www.nature.org/en-us/about-us/where-we-work/united-states/indiana/stories-in-indiana/prickly-pear-cactus/#:~:text=The%20prickly%20pear%20cactus%20is,the%20dry%20areas%20and%20hilltops.

City West, the New Chicago That Could Have Been: https://www.atlasobscura.com/places/city-west-ghost-town; https://www.nwitimes.com/news/local/newly-renovated-dunes-state-park-pavilion-unveiled/article_b117e4ae-bfc3-5246-a464-e788449dfcfa.html.

Mount Trashmore and the Lost Marsh: Kenneth Schoon's *Shifting Sands*; https://opdop.wordpress.com/2016/03/14/a-tour-of-centennial-park-in-munster-in; chicagoparent.com/things-to-do/outdoors/sledding-hills-chicago; https://www.southshorecva.com/listing/centennial-park/546; https://www.spotlightonlake.com/posts/fitness-stairs-munsters-centennial-park; https://www.chicagotribune.com/news/ct-xpm-2003-11-16-0311160079-story.html.

The Jingle Johns: https://www.nwitimes.com/business/local/watch-now-choir-of-jingle-john-porta-potties-singing-hallelujah-to-celebrate-end-of-2020/article_c910dfae-e692-550b-b266-a925fb9423e1.html; https://www.nwitimes.com/business/local/service-sanitations-jingle-john-porta-potties-rap-christmas-carols-at-lincoln-park-zoo-colts-games/article_58990dbf-655d-5eec-9747-ef34e6312925.html; https://www.nwitimes.com/entertainment/219/go/singing-porta-potties-belt-out-christmas-carols-and-go-cubs-go/article_b63310d7-0889-57f7-850c-78dca936c152.html; https://www.nwitimes.com/business/local/gary-companys-christmas-porta-potty-show-back-to-spread-holiday-cheer/article_29a30692-df16-5626-aaa9-ffb6cd18b04b.html.

Burn 'Em Brewing's Creamed Corn Beer: https://www.nwitimes.com/entertainment/50-craft-beers-of-the-south-shore-burn-em-brewings-kreamed-corn/article_b3f3a762-d866-51ca-ab1e-312f4161f06d.html; https://www.porchdrinking.com/articles/2019/05/17/burn-em-brewing-kreamed-corn; https://www.beeradvocate.com/beer/profile/35718/173873.

The Region Goes to the Movies: https://www.nwitimes.com/entertainment/movies/napoleon-dynamite-star-filming-at-lansing-bowling-alley/article_ec4f5429-c7d9-5530-ab8a-6ef7c1eb3b40.html; https://thelansingjournal.com/2018/12/05/lan-oak-lanes-stars-in-when-jeff-tried-to-save-the-world; chicagotribune.com/suburbs/daily-southtown/sports/ct-sta-tony-baranek-column-st-0921-20170920-story.html; https://digitaledition.chicagotribune.com/tribune/article_popover.aspx?guid=11a1498e-029f-427f-8ecc-da4b3f0bee10.

Straddling the Illinois-Indiana State Line: Kenneth J. Brock's *Birds of the Indiana Dunes*; https://webapps1.chicago.gov/landmarksweb/web/landmarkdetails.htm?lanId=1334

Gary Demon House: https://www.nwitimes.com/news/local/lake/portal-to-hell-lingers-in-region-priest-says/article_f9571ea9-6afa-58eb-9bce-e04dc0e7ee49.html; https://www.nwitimes.com/entertainment/television/gary-demon-house-movie-premiering-on-travel-channel-on-new-years-day/article_c50b0059-bf49-5569-8bfa-7b530592eba2.html; https://www.usatoday.com/story/news/nation/2014/01/29/alleged-demon-home-sells-for-35000/5044459; https://www.travelchannel.com/interests/haunted/articles/inside-the-bizarre-case-of-the-indiana-home-one-priest-called-a-; https://www.syfy.com/syfywire/zak-bagans-demon-house-is-still-dangerous-according-to-its-exorcisthttps://www.nwitimes.com/news/local/demon-house-movie-looks-at-whether-portal-to-hell-opened-in-gary/article_5c59b54b-e88b-53fd-b9f9-2fb41c7332c7.html

Highland Heron Rookery: http://highland.in.gov/highland-heron-rookery; https://www.birdwatchingdaily.com/hotspots/238-highland-rookery-highland-indiana; https://www.nwitimes.com/lifestyles/home-and-garden/highland-heron-rookery-attracts-majestic-birds-and-visitors/article_fa075d0a-d489-5dbb-8e1c-378224832557.html; https://www.nwitimes.com/news/local/lake/despite-some-setbacks-highland-rookery-remains-a-bird-lovers-paradise/article_0ebb9c9a-8866-5101-8983-f2906a9664fc.html.

City as Canvas: Graffiti Art in Gary: https://www.nwitimes.com/entertainment/arts-and-theatre/paintgary-project-has-splashed-color-on-abandoned-gary-buildings/article_653d4b57-cd58-54f5-9c1d-dbddf6980943.html; https://www.chicagotribune.com/suburbs/post-tribune/ct-ptb-gary-mural-st-1031-story.html; https://www.decaydevils.org/publicart; www.destinationgary.com.

Purdue Northwest Sculpture Parks: https://www.michigancitylaporte.com/see-and-do/pnw-art-collections; https://www.lpheralddispatch.com/features/article_0ac04035-00f6-5bbf-b3b5-15cb31d79678.html; https://portage.life/article/pnw-westville-campus-adds-birdman-sculpture-to-its-odyssey-sculpture-exhibit.

Brincka Cross Gardens: https://www.nwitimes.com/entertainment/columnists/eye-on-the-arts-brincka-cross-a-region-masterpiece/article_a057b9ee-d3fd-5f41-b5da-675189b86845.html; https://www.southshorecva.com/blog/post/an-artists-garden-brincka-cross-gardens-in-michigan-city; https://www.nwitimes.com/lifestyles/brincka-cross-gardens-a-lush-lovely-place-to-explore-with-acres-of-lush-gardens-and/article_e292747b-4334-575a-8bd0-ae4fb6dc31d4.html; https://panoramanow.com/events/daffodil-hike-at-brincka-cross-gardens.

Taxidermy Mountain at Cabela's: Jerome Pohlen's *Oddball Indiana*; https://www.chicagotribune.com/news/ct-xpm-2005-11-13-0511130327-story.html; https://www.roadsideamerica.com/story/9415; https://visitindiana.com/blog/index.php/2013/08/29/getting-some-beach-time-bass-pro-shopping-in-portage-indiana.

Artesian Well: https://www.usnews.com/news/best-states/indiana/articles/2021-01-24/garys-rare-artesian-spring-may-get-safer-off-road-access; https://www.chicagotribune.com/suburbs/post-tribune/ct-ptb-gary-spring-water-st-0107-20160106-story.html; https://www.wellstories.com/in/lake/chase-st-gary.

The Grande Pollution of the Grand Calumet River: https://earth5r.org/11408-2/#:~:text=The%20Grand%20Calumet%20has%20long,huge%20threat%20to%20their%20safety; https://www.wbez.org/stories/grand-calumet-river-delivers-toxic-load-to-lake-michigan/014d0456-910c-4581-9839-c354ea2efe35; https://www.indianalandmarks.org/2018/08/garys-marquette-park/

Ford Hangar in Lansing: https://www.nwitimes.com/news/local/illinois/lansing-grew-out-of-3-dutch-german-enclaves/article_a3fce1d4-91df-5052-9d77-258ba11a9a60.html; https://www.nwitimes.com/news/local/illinois/ford-tri-motor-returns-to-historic-lansing-hangar/article_4af1aed3-091b-56a4-a193-935c2fd3d1ae.html; https://www.nwitimes.com/news/local/illinois/fetching-market-returns-to-historic-ford-hangar/article_b7690df5-b638-5a10-afc1-eace0d609c62.html.

Nelson Algren Pocket Park: www.nelsonalgrenmuseumofmillerbeach.com; https://www.nwitimes.com/entertainment/books-and-literature/nelson-algren-festival-park-planned-in-garys-miller-neighborhood/article_25a98ce8-ccaf-5606-8d5c-0168e945929f.html; https://digthedunes.com/nelson-algren-event-to-take-place-in-miller-learn-a-little-about-him-and-youll-really-want-to-go.

Rensselaer Art Walk: https://www.renartwlk.org; https://www.southshorecva.com/blog/post/an-amazing-public-art-walk-in-rensselaer-indiana.

City Methodist Church: https://www.atlasobscura.com/places/city-methodist-church; https://architecturalafterlife.com/2018/10/garys-abandoned-city-methodist-church; https://substreet.org/gary-methodist.

***Wall of Crap* at Screaming Monkey Comics:** https://www.nwitimes.com/business/nwi-business-ins-and-outs-screaming-monkey-comics-smoochie-pooch-junkvets-ojs-gameover-duluth-trading/collection_64c7518f-e52c-5da3-afe3-db15ef606b3d.html; https://www.screamingmonkeycomics.com.

Giant Hobo Outside Ruben's Restaurant: https://www.roadsideamerica.com/tip/34071; https://www.nwitimes.com/news/local/lake/the-hobo-begins-new-life-in-lake-station/article_a3c7c82f-dd4f-5aa8-b515-d90b9344123d.html; https://www.nwitimes.com/news/local/local-restaurateur-minister-dies-at-73/article_06f9c2ac-e006-5beb-9d32-b32c57ddc633.html; https://www.nwitimes.com/entertainment/hot-dog-heaven/article_01cbe0d9-8530-5425-8c88-c90f0a56bb21.html.

Surfing by an Oil Refinery: Ted McClelland's *The Third Coast: Sailors, Strippers, Fishermen, Folksingers, Long-Haired Ojibway Painters and God-Save-the-Queen Monarchists of the Great Lakes*; https://southsideweekly.com/surfing-through-the-sludge-lake-michigan-us-steel; https://chicagoreader.com/news-politics/lake-surfers-say-polluted-waves-are-making-them-sick-but-they-love-it-too-much-to-stop; https://news.medill.northwestern.edu/chicago/lake-surfers-ride-the-high-frigid-waves-at-indiana-beach.

The Bailly Homestead at Indiana Dunes National Park: Kenneth J. Schoon's *Swedish Settlements on the South Shore of Lake Michigan*; https://www.nps.gov/indu/learn/historyculture/bailly_homestead.htm; https://www.indianadunes.com/explore-the-dunes/national-park/bailly-homestead-and-chellberg-farm; https://www.nwitimes.com/news/local/porter/bailly-homestead-chellberg-offer-a-glimpse-into-dunelands-past/article_3b38ef72-8200-5722-82a7-3f4605603a4a.html; https://www.nwitimes.com/news/local/porter/weekly-indiana-dunes-national-park-tour-sheds-light-on-regions-history/article_e8e0083d-9e16-5588-b819-c3eefb741b56.html.

Ideal Section of Highway: Jerome Pohlen's *Oddball Indiana*; https://www.roadsideamerica.com/story/19828; https://www.chicagotribune.com/suburbs/post-tribune/ct-ptb-bicentennial-highway-st-0911-20160909-story.html; https://www.fhwa.dot.gov/infrastructure/lincoln.cfm; https://www.in.gov/history/state-historical-markers/find-a-marker/the-lincoln-highway-the-ideal-section2; https://www.nwitimes.com/news/local/lake/1-5-mile-of-ideal-section-of-lincoln-highway-immortalized/article_d059d9c8-8a50-5ee7-a97b-981fa75af017.html.

Barker Mansion Blackout Tour: https://www.nwitimes.com/entertainment/barker-mansion-to-bring-back-blackout-tours-just-in-time-for-halloween/article_e393fdb1-4b8f-599b-859a-5fe2458c267a.html; https://www.nwitimes.com/entertainment/in-the-dark-historic-barker-mansion-hosting-blackout-tours-this-october/article_e808c016-4410-549e-b2a6-e83fee797052.html; https://panoramanow.com/historic-barker-mansion-blackout-tours-for-halloween.

Thomas Edison's Old Office: https://digitalcrossroad.com/blog/the-state-line-generating-plant-story; https://www.wrhistoricalsociety.com/the-state-line-generating-station; https://www.asme.org/about-asme/engineering-history/landmarks/24-state-line-generating-unit-1.

Candy Cane Lane: https://www.nwitimes.com/news/local/lake/a-walk-down-candy-cane-lane-c-p-street-marks-60-years-of-decorating-for/article_1fc583e2-babb-52cf-a026-320509850e45.html#:~:text=CROWN%20POINT%20%E2%80%94%20In%201958%2C%20the,known%20as%20Candy%20Cane%20Lane; https://www.nwitimes.com/news/local/lake/crown-point/view-the-lights-and-visit-candy-cane-lane/article_2ee62720-061f-5913-8aa0-f4d7497bfb76.html.

New Year's Eve Pierogi Drop: https://www.nwitimes.com/news/local/lake/whiting-ushers-new-year-in-with-pierogi-drop/article_5c0d33b3-2908-527c-9d37-72563f77d182.html; https://www.nwitimes.com/entertainment/ring-in-2018-with-whitings-pierogi-drop/article_baf5a19d-c750-54de-882f-bb26f0d7abb4.html; https://www.nwitimes.com/news/local/lake/new-years-eve-pierogi-drop-planned-in-whiting/article_c209756e-6818-5986-895f-5ef94b331c22.html.

Fighter Jet Off the Oak Savannah Trail: https://www.nwitimes.com/news/local/uncategorized/hobart-man-displays-marine-training-plane/article_a47d2dba-eeac-59b0-91a9-0139053c1292.html; https://www.traillink.com/trail/oak-savannah-trail.

Grave of Oscar Mayer's Little Oscar: https://www.nwitimes.com/news/local/jingle-whistles-all-part-of-funeral-for-little-oscar-character/article_52adbd59-37e6-540a-acd3-96652d7194c7.html; https://www.nwitimes.com/lifestyles/leisure/grave-greats-crown-point-man-finds-history-and-fascination-with-the-final-resting-places-of/article_8149e07f-0444-528b-9193-5dfb2b98126a.html; https://www.nwitimes.com/news/hotdoggers-on-a-roll-a-look-inside-the-oscar-mayer-wienermobile/article_eb380742-f0aa-522d-8975-7e2a40e97e01.html.

Florida Tropical House: Dick Wolfsie's *Indiana Curiosities*; Jerome Pohlen's *Oddball Indiana*; https://www.indianalandmarks.org/2016/09/century-of-progress-homes-indiana; https://savingplaces.org/stories/edge-of-tomorrow-the-unexpected-path-of-five-houses-of-the-future-from-the-1933-worlds-fair#.YU_vdFXMJPY; https://www.nps.gov/indu/learn/historyculture/centuryofprogress.htm; https://www.wlfi.com/content/news/Indiana-Landmarks-helps-preserve-historic-Worlds-Fair-homes-573233761.html.

Jackson Family Tribute at Hard Rock Casino: Jerome Pohlen's *Oddball Indiana*; https://wgntv.com/morning-news/chicago-scene/garys-hard-rock-casino-honors-jackson-5-indiana-music-legends-and-provides-place-for-fans-to-play; https://www.chicagotribune.com/suburbs/post-tribune/ct-ptb-gary-hard-rock-guitar-st-0409-20210408-7cukgq4ar5cjdnbqe7affl6dca-story.html; https://www.nwitimes.com/business/local/watch-now-music-memorabilia-at-new-hard-rock-casino-celebrates-jacksons-other-gary-artists/article_6fed2a55-3d74-551e-9d4d-8fbded90f539.html; https://www.mjvibe.com/the-jackson-family-museum-at-hard-rock-casino-gary-is-underway.

Edison Concept Houses: https://www.indianalandmarks.org/2016/06/set-in-concrete-edison-concept-houses; https://indianapublicmedia.org/momentofindianahistory/concrete-utopia; https://www.nwitimes.com/business/local/paintgarys-latest-murals-grab-international-art-world-recognition/article_6c4cdf3a-18ae-55d8-ac0d-a1737abdee17.html; https://www.destinationgary.com/edison-concept-houses-gary.

Nudist Clubs: Dick Wolfsie's *Indiana Curiosities*; Jerome Pohlen's *Oddball Indiana*; https://www.roadsideamerica.com/story/11825; https://www.nwitimes.com/entertainment/columnists/offbeat/nudist-colonies-local-and-from-afar-looking-for-younger-skin-and-new-members/article_da76df86-8c0e-5618-bd2c-005af9b7d026.html; https://www.nwitimes.com/uncategorized/free-to-be-me/article_82e2b723-30bc-5a0c-9cbb-25174276b1e8.html.

Former POW Camp at Sweet Woods: https://www.nwitimes.com/news/local/illinois/historical-marker-honors-ccc-site/article_3dd4e4ed-0b2b-570d-849a-03fa562151f2.html; https://www.nwitimes.com/news/local/illinois/historical-marker-dedication-is-saturday-at-former-pow-site/article_930c1dab-08c3-56ff-86d5-f87f97c19967.html; https://www.nwitimes.com/uncategorized/legacy-of-victory-1945-an-enemy-in-thorntons-midst/article_1fe642cf-6644-509c-b530-f2ebd7275b77.html; https://www.nwitimes.com/uncategorized/war-remembrances/article_7fed69cd-76bd-5c2b-a42f-14788b0ee7af.html.

Grant Street Marsh: https://indianabirdingtrail.com/pages/grant-street-marsh-birding-opportunities; http://www.dunescalaudubon.org/birding-sites.html; https://best2019festivals.com/event/indiana-dunes-birding-festival-2021-05-16-porter-in.html.

Michael Jordan Mural: https://www.nwitimes.com/business/local/artists-new-michael-jordan-mural-has-emerged-as-instant-region-landmark/article_9bf5c217-f14e-5b38-b68c-c00c5e2c7e35.html.

Beverly Shores Depot Museum and Art Gallery: https://bsdepot.org; https://www.nwitimes.com/niche/beverly-shores-museum-gallery-keep-storied-past-of-dunes-hamlet-alive/article_34f6fc2e-b1f6-535f-acba-61b60fb45295.html; https://www.nwitimes.com/entertainment/arts-and-theatre/visual/more-than-50-artists-will-display-work-at-depot-museum-and-art-gallery/article_7492a803-d683-5755-b550-c69044aa0251.html; https://www.nwitimes.com/entertainment/arts-and-theatre/beverly-shores-gallery-opens-with-strong-local-artists/article_73bd04fe-20a3-5851-b1e9-ca0093116718.html; https://www.nwitimes.com/uncategorized/a-walking-talking-history-book/article_5a589b15-9f95-5e3c-beec-90f2bf18cf57.html.

Ogden Dunes Ski Jump: Jerome Pohlen's *Oddball Indiana*; http://ogdendunes.in.gov/about-ogden-dunes/history/; https://odhistory.org/ski-jump-1927-1932; https://orangebeanindiana.com/2020/10/06/the-monstrous-ogden-dunes-ski-jump-1927-1932.

Nathan Manilow Sculpture Park: https://www.govst.edu/NMSP; https://www.chicagotribune.com/suburbs/daily-southtown/ct-sta-nathan-manilow-sculpture-park-st-0125-20210123-rlllym477zahjbj57muvvdkh2e-story.html; https://www.chicagotribune.com/suburbs/daily-southtown/ct-sta-ent-sculpture-tours-st-0924-20210916-uzezel77lfcmlgq2uzvqu6cmc4-story.html; https://www.nwitimes.com/news/local/illinois/gsu-sculpture-park-to-celebrate-35th-anniversary/article_c8b16053-e7d3-5935-bc27-824025c5f26d.html; https://www.chicagotribune.com/suburbs/daily-southtown/ct-sta-nathan-manilow-sculpture-park-st-0125-20210123-rlllym477zahjbj57muvvdkh2e-story.html.

The Ruins of Long-Abandoned Steel Mills: https://www.nps.gov/places/steelworkers-park.htm; https://beltmag.com/steelworkers-park-chicago-landscape; http://industrialscenery.blogspot.com/2020/05/steelworkers-park-and-blast-furnace.html; https://southsideweekly.com/study-south-works-stella-brown-steelworkers-park; https://www.reconnectwithnature.org/preserves-trails/preserves/joliet-iron-works-historic-site; https://www.atlasobscura.com/places/joliet-iron-and-steel-works.

Golden Age Cedar Lake at the Museum at Lassen's Resort: https://lassensresort.org; https://visitindiana.com/blog/index.php/2021/06/28/museum-on-cedar-lake; https://www.nwitimes.com/lifestyles/travel/travel-visit-museums-in-your-own-back-yard-like-the-museum-at-lassens-resort/article_c729b838-7392-532c-bbf9-4023165a7fb3.html; https://www.nwitimes.com/watch-now-cedar-lake-historical-association-harks-back-to-resort-roots-with-museum-rebranding/video_a84226d2-0c13-5b76-904c-63f3a0fdcd9a.html; https://www.nwitimes.com/news/local/historical-association-bringing-back-steamboat-tours-of-cedar-lake/article_c13fd1c6-c04e-586e-8b2d-9c9ec177c574.html.

1955 Whiting Standard Oil Refinery Explosion: John Hmurovic's *One Minute After Sunrise*; https://www.nwitimes.com/business/local/whiting-refinery-explosion-seemed-like-end-of-the-world/article_aac98d19-3240-5608-af67-8b19893b889a.html; https://www.nwitimes.com/news/local/region-museum-reopens-after-15-years/article_32169cb4-3815-51a6-be3e-0fbd7771449f.html.

Pinhook Bog in Indiana Dunes National Park: Phil Bloom's *Hiking Indiana*; https://www.nps.gov/indu/planyourvisit/pb16.htm; https://www.indianadunes.com/discover-pinhook-bog; https://www.nwitimes.com/lifestyles/home-and-garden/horror-in-the-garden-carnivorous-plants-take-a-bite-out-of-pests/article_1027f4ba-d1aa-571e-a5db-a01ba3d64bf2.html; https://www.nwitimes.com/news/local/laporte/city-of-laporte/students-learn-about-a-unique-environment-on-field-trip/article_b5e7cb18-a29e-557c-9723-53fbe4ac1beb.html.

Memorial Opera House in Valparaiso: Robert Flood's *Yesteryear Is Just Around the Corner*; Mark Skertic's *A Native's Guide to Northwest Indiana*; https://www.memorialoperahouse.com; https://www.nwitimes.com/news/history/valparaisos-memorial-opera-house-celebrates-125-years/article_548749c2-e3ba-51a4-b9fc-af7ff1176f66.html; https://www.nwitimes.com/lifestyles/20-things-you-didnt-know-about-porter-county-or-maybe-you-forgot/article_255f0584-e070-532f-8d34-b64373dbeda6.html.

***Homeless Jesus* at Valparaiso University:** https://www.nwitimes.com/news/local/porter/valparaiso/brauer-museum-of-art-at-valpo-welcomes-homeless-jesus-installation/article_501d5e5c-4aef-564a-a64b-cd24f37a0aaa.html; https://www.valpo.edu/valpomag/2019/01/30/reflecting-on-homeless-jesus-important-questions-for-reformation-day/https://www.ncregister.com/blog/a-modern-day-michelangelo-canadian-sculptor-presents-the-gospel-in-bronze.

Midwest Rail Ranger History Tour: http://www.railrangers.org; https://www.chicagotribune.com/suburbs/post-tribune/ct-ptb-south-shore-rail-rangers-st-0301-story.html; https://www.trains.com/trn/rail-rangers-educational-programs-to-resume-on-south-shore-trains.

Kingsbury Ordnance Plant in La Porte: http://www.placesthatwere.com/2017/04/kingsbury-ordnance-plant-abandoned-Ammunition-Factory.html; https://www.nwitimes.com/news/history/kingsbury-ordnance-plant-changed-the-landscape-of-laporte-county/article_24fd43de-9a15-5037-8a0c-51a0f03f73ce.html; https://orangebeanindiana.com/2019/02/14/kingsbury-ordnance; https://indianapublicmedia.org/momentofindianahistory/kingsbury-ordnance-plant; https://laportecounty.life/article/history-of-kingsbury-ordnance-plant.

Electric Car Prototype at La Porte Historical Society Museum: https://laportecountyhistory.org/exhibits/kesling-auto-collection; https://www.nwitimes.com/news/history/laporte-orthodontist-so-many-cars-each-with-its-own-story/article_0d138e31-b20c-5175-956c-258c1660071e.html; https://www.nwitimes.com/uncategorized/one-tank-trip-door-prairie-auto-museum/article_f04ef36c-1009-5d12-b981-d4d8299f7f3e.html; https://www.nwitimes.com/entertainment/driving-into-the-past/article_dc95be79-a65f-5c00-afd2-e3ad89a0a49c.html; https://www.nwitimes.com/news/local/laporte/laporte-county-builds-on-its-history-even-the-more-infamous-parts/article_bd415cb3-62de-5c09-b5ca-835b1cfff8f7.html.

Josephus Wolf House: https://www.nwitimes.com/news/local/porter/portage-highlights-its-history-in-series-of-posters-at-founders-square-park/article_0e42b9f0-d7ee-5523-904b-1f4f68ddfd6a.html; https://www.nwitimes.com/news/local/wolf-mansion-looking-for-caring-family/article_03c4cd70-5345-52b4-87c1-12393c03b38a.html; https://www.nwitimes.com/uncategorized/historic-mansion-goes-up-for-sale/article_beca2d7f-712f-5448-a43a-72cb384667b4.html; https://npgallery.nps.gov/GetAsset/99ec8748-b6ff-400d-8038-af02bf13f040.

St. Andrew the Apostle Church in Calumet City: https://liturgicalcenter.org/pl/parish-172; http://jesusshepherdofsouls.com/index.php/about; https://www.nwitimes.com/lifestyles/faith-and-values/cardinal-cupich-to-help-st-andrew-the-apostle-church-mark-125-years/article_b4b0daf3-c015-52e2-a7b6-55df39b0ba95.html.

Chicago Air and Water Show Staging Grounds: https://www.nwitimes.com/business/local/group-of-business-people-looking-to-revive-gary-air-show-that-hasnt-taken-flight-in/article_44756126-8ba2-510d-8d4c-c1a2c711f7e3.html; https://www.wbez.org/stories/garys-airport-is-takeoff-landing-hub-for-air-and-water-show/0ef880ef-bac8-425a-9bae-23215d05538a; https://www.chicagotribune.com/suburbs/post-tribune/ct-ptb-gary-air-staging-st-0817-story.html.

Hidden Fishing Pier at an International Port: https://www.nytimes.com/2019/07/17/travel/camping-hiking-indiana-dunes-national-park.html; https://www.in.gov/dnr/fish-and-wildlife/fishing/lake-michigan-fishing; https://www.chicagotribune.com/news/ct-xpm-1997-03-16-9703160316-story.html; https://www.southshorecva.com/blog/post/10-best-fishing-spots-in-northwest-indiana.

Hoosier Valley Railroad Museum: https://www.nwitimes.com/news/local/porter/valparaiso/historic-railway-car-being-refurbished-in-valpo/article_0a6cb1cb-b066-5282-94ee-da1c7baf09b2.html; https://www.nwitimes.com/news/local/hoosier-valley-railroad-museum-offers-fathers-day-excursion-train-rides/article_f156fdb2-3cf0-5cd6-8ec0-

8c28b54e6ad7.html; https://www.nwitimes.com/entertainment/all-aboard-hoosier-valley-railroad-museum-offers-train-rides-through-wooded-areas-of-nwi/article_22c8610d-744e-5864-b105-b2278284da7a.html.

No-Can-Do Pond at Sunset Hill Farm Park: https://www.portercountyparks.org/sunset-hill; https://www.nwitimes.com/news/local/new-life-as-recreation-center-means-sun-never-sets-on-sunset-hill-county-park/article_d7dc7e05-ee14-5dc2-8c84-5beda5967dce.html; https://www.nwitimes.com/uncategorized/sunset-hill-feeds-student-curiosity/article_bba270a8-cf38-5616-9ff3-8d98114b119d.html; https://www.nwitimes.com/uncategorized/putting-the-barn-back-on-sunset-hill-farm/article_6155dc44-56ee-5958-957a-fd6f915578bf.html.

Pullman National Monument: Dick Wolfsie's *Indiana Curiosities*; Jerome Pohlen's *Oddball Indiana*; https://blockclubchicago.org/2021/09/03/the-pullman-national-monument-opens-this-weekend-highlighting-the-long-history-of-the-far-south-side-neighborhood; https://chicago.suntimes.com/metro-state/2021/9/6/22659771/pullman-national-monument-opens-ribbon-cutting-mayor-lightfoot.

Calumet City Smiley Face Water Towers: https://www.nwitimes.com/uncategorized/calumet-city-couple-will-keep-their/article_dcba8517-7e59-5af0-a240-578b9ec22a1d.html; https://www.nwitimes.com/uncategorized/calumet-city-centennial-cal-city-puts-on-a-happy-face/article_08c11219-f90a-5cf5-8bcf-4be8462a681d.html; https://www.roadsideamerica.com/story/9190#:~:text=Calumet%20City%20boasts%20of%20its,Smiley%20Water%20Towers%2C%20in%201973.

Coffee Creek Watershed Nature Preserve: https://www.nwitimes.com/lifestyles/plenty-of-places-to-meditate-take-in-nature-in-region/article_96dc1248-318c-5583-8754-339c86a2484a.html; http://www.coffeecreekwc.org; https://www.nwitimes.com/lifestyles/home-and-garden/grab-a-basket-and-a-blanket-and-go-enjoy-these-picnic-perfect-sites-around-the/article_7650f44a-7d75-51e9-9817-5e98bd26dcc2.html.

Schrage Mansion and Lourdes Grotto: https://www.nwitimes.com/news/local/lake/set-in-stone-whiting-grotto-continues-to-draw-crowds-85-years-on/article_9c5ef0a8-6f7e-5cb3-94c1-a8bfb3882db6.html; https://www.nwitimes.com/business/local/newly-minted-centier-museum-bank-museum-years-in-making/article_9f35ff5e-2117-5f32-b9bb-9dd86d6bce23.html; https://www.nwitimes.com/business/local/new-centier-museum-in-downtown-whiting-adds-up-banks-rich-history/article_b58fd858-0b5c-5082-a098-4a8968da4231.html; https://www.nwitimes.com/schrage-mansion-named-to-national-register-of-historic-places/article_4ade1c9d-b724-555e-9b3c-43c1ed4b779a.html

***A Christmas Story*'s Flick Forever Licking a Flagpole at the Indiana Welcome Center:** Jerome Pohlen's *Oddball Indiana*; https://www.dailymail.co.uk/news/article-2480516/Classic-flagpole-licking-scene-A-Christmas-Story-gets-bronze-statue.html; https://www.nwitimes.com/news/local/lake/hammond/flicks-lick-from-a-christmas-story-becomes-permanent-part-of-indiana-welcome-center/article_f4dae286-da30-5714-8fdc-80909684bc6d.html; https://www.chicagotribune.com/news/ct-xpm-2013-10-29-chi-a-christmas-story-prank-to-be-immortalized-by-statue-in-hammond-20131029-story.html.

INDEX